MORE
THAN
ENOUGH

MORE THAN ENOUGH

INSPIRING MESSAGES FOR WOMEN

DESERET
BOOK

Salt Lake City, Utah

Library of Congress Cataloging-in-Publication Data

(CIP data on file)

ISBN 978-1-63993-133-0

Printed in China

RR Donnelley, Dongguan, China

10 9 8 7 6 5 4 3 2 1

CONTENTS

CONTENTS

Heavenly Father loves us, and He has incredible promises in store for us. Through scripture, He has assured us that we "are that [we] might have joy" (2 Nephi 2:25); that as His children, we can receive "all that [the] Father hath" (Doctrine and Covenants 84:38); and that through obedience, we will obtain a "fulness of joy; and . . . sit down in the kingdom of [the] Father" (3 Nephi 28:10).

These are marvelous truths. However, when we think about all that we're meant to do and become to be worthy of receiving these blessings, we may sometimes feel like we're not living up to God's expectations for us. We may even think we're the only ones who feel that way—certainly our friends and family have it figured out, even if we don't.

This book is a collection of thoughts on our divine nature and destiny from women of diverse walks of life. In it, you will find stories of hope and strategies for healing, reminding us that Heavenly Father and Jesus Christ love us perfectly *as we are*. In our trials, in our difficulties, in our weakness—and through the grace of God—we are more than enough.

WE ARE TOO MUCH

LAUREL C. DAY

I got called in to meet with my bishop after being in our new ward for just over two years. During that time we had faced some fairly significant life challenges, including the loss of my father, and as a result I had not been the most engaged member of the ward. I hadn't made much effort to get to know anyone and I often sat on the back row of Relief Society, too often letting myself slip out early. I was just struggling.

The appointment was slated for right after sacrament meeting, and it was while I was taking the sacrament that a feeling of dread came over me. I suddenly felt that I was being called to serve in Relief Society, specifically in the presidency.

Given my lack of connections in the ward as well as the space I had been in, that seemed to me to be a really bad idea. So I spent the time during the sacrament doing what any faithful woman would do: bartering with the Lord about all the reasons I was better suited for a calling in the Young Women organization.

When my husband and I sat down to meet with our bishop, my heart was pounding. As the bishop extended the call, I just started to weep. Not cry: *WEEP*—the kind of weeping where you cannot speak.

Knowing that I have a fairly demanding full-time job, and clearly seeing I was not able to respond (I'm still not sure I ever actually said yes), my good bishop proceeded to say something like, "I know this probably seems overwhelming with your schedule and travels, and I even questioned this myself at first, but it has been made clear to me that you are the woman to serve in this calling at this time."

When I *could* speak, all I was able to blurt out was: "I'm not *nice* enough to be a Relief Society president!" It was a moment of deep vulnerability, of feeling incapable of the task before me, and a time when I desperately needed validation and reassurance that I was indeed up to the job. And my good husband simply responded with, "Well . . . you have *other* gifts."

(Thank you, husband. Yes, I guess there's that.)

Simply put, I did not feel up to the challenge or the responsibility.

But as a general rule, the idea of "being enough," or rather "*not* being enough," is not something that has resonated with me. And it's not because I am not keenly aware of my inadequacies—clearly, I realize I'm not nice enough to be a Relief Society president—but rather it's that I have mostly subscribed to the thinking that my lack of "enough-ness" is simply a part of who I am. And if the Lord created me and if He loves me (both of which

I believe to be true), then that lack of "enough-ness" is nothing for me to feel overwhelmed by or ashamed of.

I think there are reasons for why I have felt this way.

I had a Primary teacher when I was younger who somehow convinced me I was Heavenly Father's favorite. I believed that deeply. So much so that there is a story in our family about a period of time when, as a young girl, I would go around our home letting my parents and siblings know that I was getting ready to say my prayers. Naturally, I assumed that Heavenly Father could only listen to one prayer at a time and, well, if His favorite was going to be praying, was there really a question which prayer He would be listening to? So I thought I was doing them a favor by giving them a heads-up.

That belief probably lasted until about the sixth grade, when middle school beat my divine confidence right out of me, as middle school is prone to do for so many of us. But even through teenage years of insecurities, my parents and my patriarchal blessing had me fairly convinced that I was *somebody* and had unique and special gifts. And so, while I was aware of what I couldn't do and the talents I didn't have, I always still believed that I was who I was supposed to be—which must have meant I was "enough."

And then perhaps because I didn't get married until I was forty-one and also didn't have children of my own, and thus never went through the overwhelming stage of being a mom, and consequently wasn't comparing myself to other moms, and therefore wasn't feeling inferior in any of those regards, I never found myself relating to so many of the things I heard women say about "not being enough." (There is something oddly nice about only comparing yourself to the kind of mom you're *pretty sure* you would have been but don't ever have to find out you weren't.)

While I was being disillusioned in my "I-don't-get-it-ness" on this topic, I felt as if the Spirit said, "Oh, Laurel, you know that thing you struggle with that you don't talk about? That thing that makes you feel like you can't get your act together and you're not strong enough? That thing that makes you feel like you're living beneath your potential?"

To which I said: "Yes. I know that thing . . . but we don't really talk about it, remember?"

To which I could imagine the Spirit saying, "Sure. But still. You know that thing? . . . *That* is what it is to feel like you're not enough."

To which I said, "Ah. I get it."

So. I get it. I do. I had been putting different words to it. But through the process of studying, I came to understand that I clearly know this feeling—this feeling that we are just not up to the tasks and responsibilities and callings before us, the feeling of coming up short. *And* I for sure understand the feeling that we are incapable of making the changes we know we need to and that somehow that lack of capacity makes us lesser than other people who seem capable of making change.

What about you? What's your "thing" that makes you feel most "not enough"? Chances are it has come to you quickly.

Now—can I share the awful truth?

We. Aren't. Enough.

We simply aren't enough for all the needs of our family.

We aren't enough for the people we've been called to serve.

I think it's safe to say we aren't enough for any of the things we've been put here on this earth to do.

And we certainly do not have enough of what we need to make the changes we often feel compelled to make in this life.

We. Are. Not. Enough. *If* we try to do any of these things on our own, without the Savior we are being encouraged to seek.

And so these feelings of "not enough" are both normal *and* a gift. And thankfully, we also have the promise of being enough in and through and because of our Savior.

Many discussions have been had about the meaning of the brief story of Mary and Martha in the book of Luke. But what if the story isn't about who chose the better part? What if it's just a glimpse into the feelings of inadequacy of one woman compared to another?

"Now it came to pass, as they went, that [Jesus] entered into a certain village: and a certain woman named Martha received him into her house. And she had a sister called Mary, which also sat at Jesus' feet, and heard his word.

"But Martha was cumbered about much serving, and came to him, and said, Lord, dost thou not care that my sister hath left me to serve alone? Bid her therefore that she help me.

"And Jesus answered and said unto her, Martha, Martha, thou art careful and troubled about many things: but one thing is needful: and Mary hath chosen that good part, which shall not be taken away from her" (Luke 10:38–42).

As I have studied this passage, I've found myself wondering: What if we're reading those verses wrong? For example, what if the verse break is in the wrong place? What if Jesus was saying, "Martha, Martha, thou art careful and troubled about many things, but one thing is needful." Period. What if that's a completely separate sentence from, "Mary hath chosen that good part"?

In other words, what if the Lord was saying, "That one thing you're doing is needful, Martha," or what if He was saying, "You are worried about so many things, but just focus on one"?

Either way, Martha was doing her thing—choosing to serve—while Mary was doing her thing—choosing to sit and listen. We don't know if that's how it always went for those two or if it was just that day. But I suspect that, considering the circumstances of the opportunity to sit and listen to Jesus, this was likely the typical routine for these two sisters. But then Martha, in what might have just been a moment of insecurity, expressed worry or frustration or resentment about what she was doing compared to Mary, and she questioned whether what she was choosing to do was "enough."

Sometimes we are Martha and sometimes we are Mary. And I worry that all too often we question our role or our choice or our effort and let our feelings of inadequacy come through. These feelings are normal.

Elder Neal A. Maxwell, in his October 1976 general conference address, said this:

"Now may I speak . . . to those buffeted by false insecurity, who, though laboring devotedly in the Kingdom, have recurring feelings of falling forever short. . . . This feeling of inadequacy is . . . normal. There is no way the Church can honestly describe where we must yet go and what we must yet do without creating a sense of immense distance. . . . This is a gospel of grand expectations."[1]

I would add that it's not just the Church describing where we must yet go and what we must yet do that creates that sense of immense distance. Sometimes it's the Church teaching the most fundamental truths about our Heavenly Father's plan that can create that sense of immense distance.

I have at times experienced that as a "single-until-I-was-forty-one-in-a-church-built-on-family-units" member. There are other ways this is felt:

Being married but not having children.

Being divorced and a single mom.

Having children "leave the fold" and choose a different path.

All of these scenarios can and do leave women sitting in sacrament meeting during baby blessings and missionary reports and a number of other things potentially feeling, sometimes deeply, these gaps. We need to be more aware of the distance some of our comments and experiences create, *and* we need to be more secure in the love of our Father in Heaven for us and our lives, especially when this "gospel of grand expectations" sometimes leaves us tempted to feel grand disappointment or grand inadequacy.

Comparing ourselves and our lives and our abilities to others, both real and perceived, is one way these feelings of inadequacy are "normal."

Another cause of feelings of inadequacy is actual failure. And that's normal too. Failure itself is normal. In fact, it's expected.

There is an obscure scripture in the Doctrine and Covenants that brings this point home.

Oliver Granger was an early convert to the Church who served several missions and then served as a member of the Kirtland high council. Joseph Smith gave Oliver the responsibility to settle the business affairs of Church leaders who had been driven out of Kirtland.

Through Joseph, this is what the Lord said to Oliver: "I remember my servant Oliver Granger; . . . and *when* he falls he shall rise again, for his sacrifice shall be more sacred unto me than his increase" (Doctrine and Covenants 117:12, 13; emphasis added).

Notice the Lord did not say "*if* he falls," He said "*when.*" Because we all will fall. We will all come up short. We will all experience failures.

Obviously we all fail at something or multiple somethings, but when that failure seems to be a repeatable offense—when we fail on the same thing again and again—feelings of inadequacy and "not enough-ness" turn into self-defeat and the temptation to give up, which is exactly what the adversary is hoping for.

Over the years, I've shared a bit about the history of my struggles with weight. I've told some stories in speaking opportunities and I blogged about it back in the day when blogging was a thing. I won't bore you with the whole history. But suffice it to say, I have read nearly every book and tried nearly every program. Some years ago, I finally felt like I had a life-changing experience losing sixty pounds and running (*and* completing) a half-marathon. I promised myself I was never going back to that other way of living. I truly believed I had changed. And then I was lucky enough to get married and have a whole new life dimension, and I got a promotion at work, and my father passed away, and—I found myself right back where I had been.

I had "failed" yet again.

And the feelings of failure and inadequacy and weakness and incapability of change began to rule and paralyze me. I was right where the adversary wanted me.

President Gordon B. Hinckley, in his October 1989 conference address entitled "Rise to the Stature of the Divine within You," said this (and please think about that title as you read this quote): "Please don't nag yourself with thoughts of failure. Do not set goals far beyond your capacity to achieve. Simply do what you can do, in the best way you know, and the Lord will accept of your effort."[2] Go ahead and read that again.

As I've gotten older, I have also come to believe that these feelings are a gift to help me progress.

Sister Michelle D. Craig, in her October 2018 general conference address, "Divine Discontent," said this perfectly:

"Each of us, if we are honest, feels a gap between where and who we are, and where and who we want to become. We yearn for greater personal capacity. We have these feelings because we are daughters and sons of God, born with the Light of Christ yet living in a fallen world. These feelings are God-given and create an urgency to act.

"We should welcome feelings of divine discontent that call us to a higher way, while recognizing and avoiding Satan's counter-feit—paralyzing discouragement. . . .

"The surprising truth is that our weaknesses can be a blessing when they humble us and turn us to Christ."[3]

I can see in my own life that when I am experiencing these feelings of inadequacy, *God is trying to do something for me and He is stirring my heart to become something more.* It's uncomfortable, but because I believe this, I welcome it.

C. S. Lewis, in *Mere Christianity,* says it this way in this classic quote: "Imagine yourself as a living house. God comes in to rebuild that house. At first, perhaps, you can understand what He is doing. He is getting the drains right and stopping the leaks in the roof and so on: you knew that those jobs needed doing and so you are not surprised. But presently He starts knocking the house about in a way that hurts abominably and does not seem to make any sense. What on earth is He up to? The explanation is that He is building quite a different house from the one you thought of— throwing out a new wing here, putting on an extra floor there, running up towers, making courtyards. You thought you were being made into a decent little cottage: but He is building a palace. He intends to come and live in it Himself."[4]

I know sometimes it might feel like God bought the house and just demolished it because what He really wanted was the piece of land so He could start all over. But if we are willing to let Him—truly let Him—come and take ownership, or be a co-investor in the property, if you will, He can make more of our life and our weaknesses than we ever could on our own. So why would we want to stand in the way of *that?*

I think intellectually we wouldn't, but still sometimes it's painful and a little scary to go down that road with Him. In fact, sometimes even when He's been willing to show us a glimpse of the blueprint for the new home He is intending to build, we still resist with crippling discouragement that can sometimes cause us to withdraw—or worse, to shirk from something He has asked us to do.

Such was the case with Moses when he questioned his ability to answer the call to lead the Israelites:

"And Moses said unto the Lord, O my Lord, I am not eloquent, neither heretofore, nor since thou hast spoken unto thy servant: but I am slow of speech, and of a slow tongue. And the Lord said unto him, Who hath made man's mouth? or who maketh the dumb, or deaf, or the seeing, or the blind? have not I the Lord? Now therefore go, and I will be with thy mouth, and teach thee what thou shalt say" (Exodus 4:10–12).

That's a pretty sweet promise from the Lord, yet Moses still resists and tries to offer another suggestion (kind of like me when I tried to barter to be in the Young Women program). He still suggests the Lord use someone else:

"And he said, O my Lord, send, I pray thee, by the hand of him whom thou wilt send. *And the anger of the Lord* was kindled *against Moses,* and he said, Is not Aaron the Levite thy brother? I know that he can speak well. And also, behold, he cometh forth to meet thee: and when he seeth thee, he will be glad in his heart. And thou shalt speak unto him, and put words in his mouth: and I will be with thy mouth, and with his mouth, and will teach you what ye shall do" (Exodus 4:13–15; emphasis added).

I can imagine it might frustrate the Lord because He is well aware of what He is planning to do for us and how we are attempting to alter that plan. But fortunately for all of us, our Father in Heaven is a loving and patient Father—and His plan allows for our slow and hesitant progress.

Several months ago, I began to get a stirring—a "divine discontent," as Elder Maxwell and more recently Sister Craig have spoken about. The only way I can describe it is a loving invitation to try again.

My husband and I, as part of my path back to health, recently spent a week at a health and fitness "resort." (I use that term loosely because really, when you're participating in a program that has you doing 25,000 steps and burning 4,500 calories in a day but only eating 1,200 calories—albeit delicious ones—can it *really* be called a resort?)

Early one morning, during one of the hikes, I was thinking about the many ways I have fallen short these past several years and experiencing the feelings of regret we have when we know we've held ourselves back. I said within myself, "I am just not where I could be."

And at the risk of leading you to believe I hear complete

sentences from the Spirit all the time (which I don't), the next thought I had was: "Are you *moving* closer to me?"

I got a little emotional for a minute and knew I could answer yes.

And then, I felt, as strongly as I have felt anything, this response: "Then that is enough."

My dear friends, when our desire is that we are enough, when we are willing to show up and give *some* effort, even if it seems so small, we are doing enough. We have to trust that we are.

Because the truth is that the space between our mortal inadequacy and His call for our lives *can* and WILL be filled. He makes it ENOUGH.

I love this passage in Exodus 36. The Israelites have been commanded to build a tabernacle—not an easy task. But look at these three verses:

"And they [the wise men whom the Lord had called to lead the building of the tabernacle] spake unto Moses, saying, The people bring *much more than enough* for the service of the work, which the Lord commanded to make. And Moses gave commandment, and they caused it to be proclaimed throughout the camp, saying, Let neither man nor woman make any more work for the offering of the sanctuary. So the people were restrained from bringing. For the stuff they had was sufficient for all the work to make it, and too much" (vv. 5–7).

Do you see it? More importantly, *do you feel it?* When we are in partnership with the Lord—when we are responding to the call

He has extended to us to serve and teach and lead and even to change, *the stuff we have is sufficient and too much.*

But how? How is this possible?

In his second epistle to the Corinthians, Paul says, "Not that we are sufficient of ourselves to think any thing as of ourselves; but our sufficiency is of God" (2 Corinthians 3:5).

The stuff we have is sufficient and too much because our sufficiency is of God. And what is that sufficiency?

Sister Craig continues in her talk: "The good news of the gospel is that with *the grace* of God, we *are* enough. *With Christ's help,* we can do all things."[5]

Without Him, we are not enough. But with Him and through His grace, we are exactly enough. In fact, we are more than enough. Or as the scripture said, "too much."

His grace is sufficient—His grace is ENOUGH.

Again to the Corinthians, Paul taught: "And [the Lord] said unto me, My grace is sufficient for thee: for my strength is made perfect in weakness" (2 Corinthians 12:9).

His grace fills in the gaps in remarkable ways; ways that I promise each of us have experienced—whether we have recognized it as such or not. And when He does that for us, it is a beautiful thing to behold and to feel.

That thing you identified earlier? What would you need God to do in your life in order for you to be ENOUGH for the call or the challenge you identified? And do you believe that He can and will? If you don't, pray for that. Don't pray for the help just yet. Pray that you can believe that He can and will.

Are you familiar with the story in the Old Testament of the Ammonites coming to attack the kingdom of Judah? It is found in 2 Chronicles 20.

The king, Jehoshaphat, was afraid when he heard the Ammonites were coming, and he invited all the people in the kingdom to fast and gather together to pray to the Lord for help. Jehoshaphat stood in the midst of the congregation and cried unto the Lord, "O our God, . . . we have no might against this great company that cometh against us; neither know we what to do: but our eyes are upon thee. And all Judah stood before the Lord, with their little ones, their wives, and their children. Then upon Jahaziel . . . , a Levite . . . , came the Spirit of the Lord in the midst of the congregation; and he said, . . . Thus saith the Lord unto you, Be not afraid nor dismayed by reason of this great multitude; *for the battle is* not yours, but God's. . . . Ye shall not need to fight in this battle: *set yourselves, stand ye still,* and *see* the salvation of the Lord with you" (vv. 12–15, 17).

And then the Lord did just that. They prepared for battle and, instead of having to fight, the Lord sent other armies to come upon the Ammonites and destroy them.

But whether they fought or not was not the point. The Lord took what they did have to offer and He made them enough. And again, that's what He does for us.

Think about the counsel He gave them and apply it to your own "not enough-ness":

"Set yourselves." Or in other words, show up with what you have.

"Stand still." Or in other words, don't get overwhelmed. Stand still and trust Him.

"And see the Lord's grace work in you." I love that it doesn't say "look for." The Lord said, "SEE the Lord's grace work in you." You will see it because it WILL.

Remember, grace, provided in and through Jesus Christ, fills the gap between our ability and what we've been called to do. We were created to be all that He needs and wants us to be. We are capable of being *enough* in all we are asked to do and in every weakness we want to overcome.

With Jesus, whom we seek, you have enough and you ARE enough. Yea verily, you are more than enough—even "too much."

That is my promise. That is HIS promise.

Notes

1. Neal A. Maxwell, "Notwithstanding My Weakness," *Ensign*, November 1976.
2. Gordon B. Hinckley, "Rise to the Stature of the Divine within You," *Ensign*, November 1989.
3. Michelle D. Craig, "Divine Discontent," *Ensign*, November 2018.
4. C.S. Lewis, *Mere Christianity* (2015), 205.
5. Michelle D. Craig, "Divine Discontent"; emphasis added.

THE BEAUTIFUL REALITY OF WHAT IT MEANS TO BE A DAUGHTER OF GOD

BONNIE CORDON, MICHELLE CRAIG,
AND BECKY CRAVEN

Sister Becky Craven: My good friend told me a story about something that happened to her daughter, Tiffany, when she was sixteen years old.

Just a few months after receiving her driver's license, and while driving home after a Young Women activity one evening, Tiffany was stopped by a police officer because of a burned-out taillight. This was the first time that she had been pulled over, so you can probably imagine how extremely nervous she was! The officer asked her for her driver's license and registration. But Tiffany had left her purse at the church. And after cleaning out the car earlier that week, she had forgotten to put the registration back in the glove box.

So after several questions from the police officer, and very nervous responses from Tiffany, the officer finally asked, "Do you even know who you are?"

Tiffany, by then, was in tears, but she responded, "Yes, I am a daughter of my Heavenly Father who loves me, and I love Him."

I wish that each of us had such a knowledge of our divine identity as Tiffany. Before she could even remember to say her own given name, she first declared her identity as a daughter of God. Do we remember who we are, always? Is it instinctive? Is it set in our nature?

In the Young Women theme, we boldly declare our daughterhood of Heavenly Parents, for as the scriptures teach, "We are the offspring of God" (Acts 17:29).

Although the veil is currently drawn between present and past memories, I believe that eternal truths are stored within our souls.

When my parents joined the Church as a young couple, the principles and doctrines taught to them by the missionaries were familiar to them, although they had never been taught in the churches they had previously attended. My mother recently told me that when she learned about eternal families, it was as if a forgotten truth returned to her memory.

In the premortal Council in Heaven, we chose our Heavenly Father's plan. We stood by Jesus Christ with full confidence and trust that He would do for us what He said He would do, to help us return to our heavenly home. We chose to come to earth and receive a physical body so that we could eventually become like our Heavenly Parents.

So why is it so important for us to remember these truths? Why does it even matter? Because when we know who we are:

- it amplifies our understanding of what we can become, and it gives us a standard by which to live;
- it helps us to live our covenants and emulate Christlike characteristics;
- and it propels us to treat others as daughters and sons of God and shun divisive thoughts and behaviors.

Understanding our divine heritage gives us strength to prevail over the adversary and sustain us through the challenges of life. It gives us an eternal perspective. And I'm sure you can think of other blessings that come from knowing that you are a divine daughter of Heavenly Parents.

But Satan is cunning, and he presents us with distractions that cause us to forget who we are and our eternal value. In Greek mythology, we learn the story of the Trojan War and the Greeks' very well-formulated plan to overtake and destroy the city of Troy. As most of the Greek forces pretended to retreat, a few soldiers hid inside a gigantic hollow wooden horse that was placed outside the city gates of Troy. And thanks to some well-placed lies, the Trojans believed the horse to be a gift and dragged it into their city. But once inside the city walls, the hidden soldiers emerged from the wooden horse, opened the city gates to the Greek forces, and laid waste to Troy.

Like the Trojan horse, what deceptions and distractions does Satan place before us to minimize our identity and self-worth? What stands in our way of reaching our divine potential? What Trojan horses do we need to unmask?

It is a blessing to know who we are. For me personally, it gives me courage to stretch beyond my natural abilities to do things I never thought I could do. It helps me to stay grounded in a world with conflicting attitudes and views. And it gives me confidence to face the future with faith.

Sister Michelle D. Craig: We live in a world of twenty-four-hour news feeds and conflicting messages from all sides.

If we're not careful, these messages can cause us to doubt our divine nature or to forget the good news Jesus came to share with His disciples.

One summer I was walking on a path not far from my home and a woman walked past me going the other direction. She looked at me—and then she looked twice. I smiled and said hello and kept walking. And she called out to me after I passed—"You look really familiar; do you do the news?"

I didn't think fast enough, but I wished I would have said, "Yes! I love to talk about the good news of the gospel!"

It is good news! We are beloved daughters of Heavenly Parents. God loves us, and as disciples of Jesus Christ, we strive to become like Him. And in our striving, we are loved.

We are all in different stages of life, but we are united in our desires to become more like Jesus Christ. This process of discipleship is not a checklist; it is individual, and it doesn't happen quickly! But let's just start right where we are, which is always where discipleship starts—right where we are.

Love God

When we love God with our hearts, our minds, and with all of our strength, we can do hard things.

I am learning that the Lord is more concerned with my growth as a disciple than He is about my comfort. I don't know about you, but I really like my comfort zone! I remember my son writing home from his mission that while he was praying one day he felt an impression to "leave his comfort zone and get into the Comforter's zone." That is a profound thought.

If we want to be disciples, we will certainly be asked to do some things that are hard, some things that take us right beyond ourselves and into the "Comforter's zone."

These things don't have to be big and flashy; they will most often be small things, but we can do them with great love. "By this shall all men know that ye are my disciples, if ye have love one to another" (John 13:35). Even if we are weak and flawed, this is a path open to all disciples.

Love Others

My daughter has a good friend whose mother was battling cancer. As a last resort, this woman and her husband flew to China to receive treatments. Some sweet Chinese sisters who lived in a distant branch of the Church heard they had a Relief Society sister from America who was suffering. They sprang into action. Rather than waiting for an official assignment or a sign-up sheet to be passed around, these sisters followed a prompting to serve—a prompting that was probably a bit uncomfortable. They traveled for hours on buses to visit a sister, a sister who did not speak their language, but who could surely understand their love. These sisters did what they could to bring comfort. They rubbed her feet with oils, and they came day after day until Sister Reilly passed. This is one example of what it looks like to be a disciple of Jesus Christ, who taught us that He came to earth to serve others (see Matthew 20:28). These women served with great love.

Disciples can show this great love in small acts: by opening your home and your heart to one who might be wandering; by loving others you work with—whether that work is changing diapers or changing minds. Discipleship looks like not suppressing a generous thought. It looks like accepting Church callings that overwhelm or underwhelm and paying a full tithe when there is more month than money. It is trusting God and His timing when you find yourself in a waiting place. It is an awareness that though our circumstances may not change, our characters can, our hearts can, and in the end, that is all that really matters.

We Are Loved

And finally, as disciples of Jesus Christ, we know that we are loved, and we know that sometimes it's okay to feel broken, because we worship One who will make us whole.

Jesus Christ heals broken things. We are all broken in some way—broken hearts, broken dreams, broken bodies, broken minds—and that's okay. Jesus Christ welcomes us in our brokenness and in our desire to become His disciples. Perhaps that is one reason He retains the marks of His wounds, even after His

Resurrection—to remind of us the wounds He bore for us and the promise that He will heal ours (see 3 Nephi 11:13–15). He is the Master Healer. He extends His grace in abundance, allowing us to heal, allowing our capacity to be enlarged and our shoulders strengthened to carry the burdens placed upon them. His grace heals, and we can be better and stronger because we come broken to our Savior and our Redeemer. Because we are loved.

I am sure that Jesus would say to women of covenant living today, as He said to the faithful when He was in the Americas: "Ye are my disciples, and ye are a light unto this people" (3 Nephi 15:12).

We are beloved daughters, we are disciples, and we are to be witnesses of His love—and that is glorious.

Sister Bonnie H. Cordon: There is a comforting power that comes as we understand our *identity* and *purpose* as covenant women of God. A miracle can occur as we let that deep divine understanding shine from ourselves to others—that invitation and covenant to stand as a witness of God (see Mosiah 18:9).

I don't know about you, but for me, there are times when "witnessing" feels a little daunting. Do I know enough? Do I have the right words? My life feels a little messy to be an example for anyone.

As I ponder this, I think of an experience one morning, not long ago. I found myself in my office before dawn. The dark sky seemed to emphasize the chaos and construction happening around the Salt Lake Temple. As I stood there focused on the broken, and messy, and the damaged rubble, the stillness of the early hours brought a peace to my soul and my focus shifted upward. A quiet thought filled my mind: "The light is still shining!" The temple's structure may be in disarray for now, but the beacon of the temple is no less effective. In fact, to me it stands as a powerful message due to the current imperfection while in the process of being improved and fortified.

We may personally feel like we are under construction, like the chaos and debris of our lives is on display for all to see—but *your light is still shining!* Our source of light, our Savior, is unwavering! The bits and pieces strewn about are the evidence of our personal renovation—these make you unique, interesting, resilient, and beautiful! They are evidence of your effort to strengthen your faith. As Captain Moroni said of his people, "The Lord is with us . . . because of our . . . faith in Christ . . . [and] *ye cannot destroy this our faith*" (Alma 44:3; emphasis added).

I love that even in the midst of our mortal remodel the Lord asks us to "stand as witnesses of God at all times and in all things, and in all places" (Mosiah 18:9). He doesn't give us any qualifiers. He doesn't say when the house is clean, when the children are at their angelic best, or when work finally calms down. He asks us to witness of Him *now*.

Let me share a story of someone who let her light shine and stood as a witness in the middle of a personal remodel—a change in work assignment.

When Lori received this new responsibility at work, she altered her daily routine. She admitted that "whether for dietary or emotional reasons," she went to Chick-fil-A every single day for lunch. She became acquainted with many of the employees and felt drawn to a server named Melissa. Melissa was delightful, and she had one of those laughs that was a burst of joy. Lori and Melissa quickly connected. What they didn't know was that the Lord had something much more in mind.

Even with all that was going on in Lori's life, she felt the prompting to make room for a new friend. She soon learned that Melissa had grown up in the Church but had started making choices in her teenage years that had taken her away. At Lori's invitation, Melissa agreed to go to sacrament meeting *after twenty years of being away.*

What came next was a series of small but meaningful steps as these new friends walked the covenant path together. Melissa started attending church. She and Lori studied the Book of Mormon together. Despite many roadblocks and trials, they pressed forward with faith in Jesus Christ. Melissa took the sacrament again, paid her tithing; she even had the chance to teach Relief Society. After a two-year journey of faith, Lori had the privilege of standing by Melissa's side as her escort when she entered the temple for the first time. From a chance meeting over a lunch order to the house of the Lord, that miraculous day is one of those mortal moments that forever carries a heavenly spotlight for these two faithful women. They share a steadfast witness of the Savior's healing power and a renewed conviction of our Father's love for His children!

Admittedly, that part in the Lord's invitation about "all times," "all things," and "all places" can be very overwhelming.

We won't be perfect, and that's okay. But we can *strive,* and thankfully we can repent as needed. Let me share a personal tutoring example.

Now, I will admit that I often move "with haste" from one thing to another, with just minutes to spare before being late. It was one of those kinds of days in Brazil, when my husband and I were serving as mission leaders. We had a mission conference and had stopped by a local grocery store to grab some drinks for the missionaries who were attending. There we were, in the checkout line with eighty-five cans of soda. Our cashier appeared to be new. She picked up the first can of soda, carefully scanned it, and set it down softly enough to preserve every bubble of carbonation. She then picked up the next soda and the next, *slowly* repeating the process. My mind was screaming, "Are you kidding me?!" But I was so proud that not a single murmur escaped my lips. I had my missionary tag on, after all. It was then that my husband's hand tapped my arm and he raised his eyebrows, as he does so well.

"What?" I hadn't said anything!

"Your eyes said it all," he quietly responded.

Perhaps this is, in part, what is meant by the sacred promise to "always remember Him" (Moroni 4:3; 5:2). Reflecting the love of our Savior not only through our words, but our eyes. Witnessing includes how we see people, treat them, and help them.

The Lord asks us to be a light, to be a witness. We can do this because we do not do it alone. The lives of those around us are precious to our Heavenly Father. He invites us to link our hearts with His and treat all with love—His love.

The Lord has called us to "Rise, and stand upon thy feet . . . to make thee a *minister* and a *witness*." Why? "To open their eyes and to turn them from darkness to light, and from the power of Satan unto God" (Acts 26:16, 18; emphasis added). It is more than just kindness. I think of it as kindness in Christ—that power that comes when your goodness is combined with the promise of exaltation through our merciful and loving Savior.

No matter the rubble that may surround your feet, no matter the mess you feel you are in, look up! The light of the gospel of Jesus Christ shines through you for those around you. The Lord's light is more than enough. *You are enough.* Stand tall, and shine on.

HAVING EYES, EARS, AND HEARTS TO GATHER SAFELY IN CHRIST

ROSEMARY THACKERAY

I am a gatherer. It is in my DNA. My parents were gatherers. They relished the opportunity to join together with friends and family, usually with an abundance of food. We often made room for extra people around our kitchen table. It was my uncle for noonday lunch when the brothers were working cattle. Our Thanksgiving dinner, with turkey and all the trimmings, including made-from-scratch hot rolls and pie, was shared with individuals who had no family or place to go. And for many years, every Sunday evening friends came by for homemade ice cream and freshly baked chocolate chip cowboy cookies.

Most of us enjoy gathering. One lesson we learned from the COVID-19 pandemic is that human interaction is vital to our mental and emotional health. It was not easy for us to follow the rules to stay home and stay safe, to keep six feet apart from other people, to greet each other without an embrace or handshake, and limit our gatherings to immediate family. We missed congregating for Sunday worship, participating in temple ordinances to gather our ancestors, and meeting to celebrate weddings, funerals, birthdays, baptisms, and more.

A well-known gathering parable is found in the New Testament—it is the story of the wedding feast (see Luke 14:16–24; Matthew 22:2–10). The king has prepared a great meal to honor his son's marriage. He extends the invitations. People begin to send their regrets saying they are unable to attend. The food is ready, the time for celebration has arrived, but there are no guests. The king sends his servants into the streets to invite others to come and join the supper. In Revelations 19:9, referring to this event, it reads: "Blessed are they which are called unto the marriage supper of the Lamb."

You and I are invited to this feast by Jesus Christ, the master Gatherer. Christ refers to himself as the Good Shepherd. Shepherds gather their sheep to the fold. Jehovah, the Lord of the Old Testament, covenanted with ancient Israel that He would gather in His people (see Ezekiel 34:13; Isaiah 11:12).

I would like to share four truths that can help us respond to Christ's invitation to gather to Him and increase our ability to gather scattered Israel as we prepare the world for the Savior's Second Coming.

Truth number one: He knows you.

He knows you and He knows your name.

Jesus Christ not only calls the stars by their name (see

Psalm 147:4), but He knows and calls His sheep—you and me—by our names (see John 10:3).

We read in the scriptures when Moses, Enoch, Enos, Joseph Smith, and others were called by name. If the Lord knew these people by name, then we have confidence that He knows us also.

He knows each of us individually—not collectively as a group of His children. He knows our innermost thoughts. The desires of our heart. Our dreams. Our disappointments.

He knows each of us one by one.

He knows I like ice cream—and that Aggie lemon custard and Ben and Jerry's Chubby Hubby are my favorite flavors.

He knows I'd rather sleep in a hotel than go camping in the mountains—but I went to Young Women camp anyway.

He knows I have no sense of direction and can easily get lost.

He knows I sometimes mourn the missed opportunity to have been a wife and mother.

When my nephew Justin was five years old, he started exhibiting behaviors that were concerning for my sister Laura and her husband Mark. For example, he forgot how to pull up a zipper on his jacket, he would stumble walking up the school bus steps, when washing his hands he said he could not see the soap on the bathroom sink, and he became increasingly ill for no apparent reason. Laura reached out to her pediatrician. The doctor suggested Justin had just started school, so he was likely experiencing separation anxiety being away from his mother.

One Sunday afternoon, Laura's family and I were visiting my parents. Usually Justin would eagerly respond to my invitation to walk to the school playground for a few rides on the swing. That day he was not interested. He said, "I just want to stay with my mom." As we gathered around the kitchen table eating lunch, Justin had a faraway look in his eyes. A somber feeling permeated the house. Laura, Mom, and I sat on the living room couch, the warm afternoon sun streaming in the windows as we tenderly discussed Justin's situation. We gently wiped away tears as they trickled down our cheeks.

The next morning when I arrived at work, I picked up the telephone and called Laura. I can still remember exactly where I was standing in my office in the Richards Building on the campus of Brigham Young University. I said to her, "Laura, I know you are the mom, but there is something seriously wrong with Justin."

In a quivering voice full of emotion, she quietly responded, "I know."

I encouraged her to call Sandy, a relative who was a doctor. Within a few hours Justin was in Sandy's office, where he immediately made a diagnosis. Sandy sent Laura and Justin home for brain scans at the local hospital. The next day Justin was at Primary Children's Hospital in Salt Lake City, Utah, meeting with two surgeons. One of the surgeons was not supposed to be on call that day, but he was, and not by coincidence, he was a brain tumor expert and familiar with this rare astrocytoma. On Wednesday, a shunt was inserted into Justin's head to drain the accumulated fluid.

On Friday, the surgeons performed an eight-hour surgery,

removing as much of the brain tumor as they could without destroying Justin's vision.

Because Jesus Christ knows you and me, we can trust Him to help us. He knows what assistance we need and when it would be best for us to receive that support. He knows how and when to reach out and succor us.

In John 10:14 it reads: "I am the good shepherd, and know my sheep, and am known of mine."

The Savior knows us. The question for us is—do we know Him? Knowing the Lord is required for us to be gathered and eventually receive eternal life (see Doctrine and Covenants 29:27).

The Savior added: "And if they know me they shall come forth, and shall have a place eternally at my right hand" (Mosiah 26:24).

Elder David A. Bednar stated the following about how we can come to know the Lord:

> A grand objective of mortality is not merely learning about the Only Begotten of the Father but also striving to know Him. Four essential steps that can help us come to know the Lord are exercising faith in Him, following Him, serving Him, and believing Him.[1]

As we come to know the Savior, our desire to reach out and gather others in love, just as He would, increases.

I invite all of us to consider what we can do to know the Savior better than we do today.

Truth number two: He hears you.

In the Book of Mormon, the Savior commanded the Nephites, and us today, to always pray unto the Father in His name (see 3 Nephi 18:19).

I am confident that each of you could share an experience when you prayed and God heard you and answered you. It may have been when you poured out your soul to Him in audible prayer. Or it may have been a silent prayer offered in a public place. Or a prayer you held in your heart for years.

I now return to Justin's story. As I drove home from my parents' that October evening, reflecting on Justin's situation, I had a distinct impression come into my mind—I either believed that when I prayed, God heard and answered my prayers, or He did not. The time to develop faith was past.

During the next few days, weeks, and months, I prayed frequently, sincerely, and earnestly for Justin's health and recovery. I know from personal experience that not all prayers are answered in the way we would like or in the time we prefer. We pray, we petition, we wait upon the Lord.

Today Justin is a healthy, happy, talented, and kind young man. Justin's life is a miracle. He is a reminder to us that Heavenly Father and Jesus Christ are in the details of our lives. They were, and are, mindful of Justin and his situation. They knew what he was experiencing and what medical assistance he needed at that exact moment, and who would be able to provide that care.

God hears us when we pray. The question for us is—do we hear and know the Good Shepherd's voice?

The ability to hear the Lord's voice is an indication that we are His disciples. After King Benjamin's people made a covenant to take upon themselves Christ's name and obey His commandments, King Benjamin admonished them to both *know* and *hear* the voice by which they were called (see Mosiah 5:8, 12).

Ministering to others in ways that are uniquely suited to them is one way we participate in gathering. As we increase our capacity to hear Jesus Christ's voice, we are able to receive promptings for how we can best serve others.

One day at church my friend Kathryn received a prompting to take a meal to a lady sitting a few rows in front of her. Kathryn approached the woman and offered her services. The woman indicated they were moving that week and the meal would be greatly appreciated. During the conversation, Kathryn asked if the woman's mother would be helping her family move. In response, the woman said she had recently passed away. Kathryn then received an impression from the Spirit—it was this woman's mother who was asking for someone to please help her daughter.

Kathryn responded to a quiet prompting and helped a sister feel encircled in Christ's love.

Sometime later, Kathryn prayed one morning to feel her own deceased mother's presence and recognize her influence. That day, a neighbor appeared at her doorstep with a pan of sweet rolls— just like her mother used to make.

Hearing the Good Shepherd's voice allows Christ to gather us and allows us to safely gather others to Him.

Truth number three: He sees you.

Perhaps there have been times you have felt insignificant, even invisible. It may have seemed that nobody, including God, was aware of you. Even Joseph Smith cried out in Liberty Jail, "O God, where art thou? And where is the pavilion that covereth thy hiding place?" (Doctrine and Covenants 121:1).

The truth is, the Lord sees us, even though we cannot see Him.

In Doctrine and Covenants 38:7 we read: "But behold, verily, verily, I say unto you that mine eyes are upon you. I am in your midst and ye cannot see me."

It seems that when we feel little or no control over our circumstances, that is when we earnestly seek an affirmation that the Lord sees us and is aware of our situation. That is how I felt last summer when both my parents were experiencing failing health. My dad was diagnosed with cancer followed by the discovery of a volleyball-size tumor on his kidney. My mom had several health challenges, all of which were compounded by advanced dementia, which seemed to progress exponentially with my dad's declining health. I was starting a new position at work, my schedule would be more demanding, and I was anxious about how my three siblings and I would care for Mom once our dad passed away.

During this time, my friend Brad shared with me his experience from when his mom was dying from lung cancer just a few years earlier. He said:

> I prayed to ask Heavenly Father to relieve my mom's burden. The thought came to me that my mom was in His

hands and care, and that my responsibility was to be faithful to Him and to my mom. It was a sobering experience for me. I was reminded that the Lord is not in some distant galaxy far away from us. He is near to us and in the details of our lives. He knows and controls when it is time for us to return to Him.

One day I went to the temple with the purpose of seeking an answer to a course of action for my mom. As I waited to participate in the ordinances, I was seated next to a beautiful painting of a young girl with long blonde hair cascading over her shoulders. She sat in a bright green pasture against a clear blue sky, with flowers in bloom all around her. I thought of my mom. When she was a young girl, she had long blonde hair; she wore it in braids. She found joy in flowers and gardening. The impression came that many family members were waiting on the other side of the veil to greet her. As I spent time pondering, I picked up the scriptures and the pages fell open to Doctrine and Covenants 44:6, which reads:

> Behold, I say unto you, that ye must visit the poor and the needy and administer to their relief, that they may be kept until all things may be done according to my law which ye have received.

My answer was—I just needed to keep visiting Mom and doing what I could to relieve her suffering. As Brad had said, the Lord was mindful of us and of Mom's situation. Five days later Dad passed away. In the early morning hours on the day of Dad's funeral, Mom quietly crossed the veil to be reunited with her sweetheart. My prayers were answered, and her burden was lifted.

The Savior sees us. How often do we *look for Jesus* in our life?

In the scriptures the prophets repeatedly admonish us to remember the goodness of God (see Mosiah 4:11–12). Likewise, we are commanded to thank the Lord in all things (see Doctrine and Covenants 59:7). There are many blessings that come from following this counsel. One key blessing is the ever-present gift of His Spirit to be with us. The Spirit will guide our journey back to God.

Truth number four: He loves you.

President Dieter F. Uchtdorf stated:

> Our Savior, the Good Shepherd, knows and loves us. He knows and loves you. He knows when you are lost, and He knows where you are. He knows your grief. Your silent pleadings. Your fears. Your tears. It matters not how you became lost—whether because of your own poor choices or because of circumstances beyond your control. What matters is that you are His child. And He loves you. He loves His children.[2]

The Savior loves us. Do we love Him?

If we love God with all our might, mind, and strength, we are promised that His grace is sufficient for us.

In Hebrew, the root word for grace is *chanan* (khaw-nan), which means to bend or stoop in kindness. What a powerful image. Because of His Atonement, Christ is bending down, or stooping in kindness, to help us through our challenges in life.

When we love the Savior, we, in turn, extend charity, the pure love of Christ to others—we love without judgment, or conditions, or any expectations of love in return.

Elder Jeffrey R. Holland suggested that one day we will individually report on our love for God:

> My beloved brothers and sisters, I am not certain just what our experience will be on Judgment Day, but I will be very surprised if at some point in that conversation, God does not ask us exactly what Christ asked Peter: Did you love me? I think He will want to know if in our very mortal, very inadequate, and sometimes childish grasp of things, did we at least understand one commandment, the first and greatest commandment of them all—Thou shalt love the Lord thy God with all thy heart, and with all thy soul, and with all thy strength, and with all thy mind.[3]

I invite us all to make a conscious effort to develop a testimony of these simple truths. It will be a quest of a lifetime to come to know the Savior, to hear Him, to see and recognize His hand in our lives, and to demonstrate our love for Him.

Having a conviction deep down in our hearts that the Lord knows us, sees us, hears and loves us, will change our lives. We will know why we are here and how we should be spending our time. Our confidence will increase. We will not be swayed by the opinions and philosophies of the world.

It is our work to respond to the invitation to help gather scattered Israel and prepare for the Savior's Second Coming.

President Russell M. Nelson has indicated: "This gathering is the greatest challenge, the greatest cause, and the greatest work on earth today!"

To the sisters he specifically said, "We need you! . . . We need your strength, your conversion, your conviction, your ability to lead, your wisdom, and your voices."[4]

When these four truths are written in the fleshy tables of our hearts, we will care less about what people think about us, including how many likes or followers we have on our social media accounts. The Lord's love is deeper and more enduring than any fleeting praise and adoration the world has to offer.

Knowing the Lord has our back will give us the courage and confidence to face any trials that will come our way. When our foundation is the Lord, Jesus Christ, the devil may send forth his winds, but they will have no power to drag us down to the gulf of misery and endless woe (see Helaman 5:12).

Several years ago, I was earnestly seeking an answer to a life question. One Sunday I approached the Lord in fasting and prayer. I determined to end my fast after I met with the stake presidency to be set apart for a calling. During the setting apart, the blessing I received was beautiful, but my question remained unanswered. At the conclusion of the meeting the stake president invited me to remain after the other seven or eight people left the room. He then told me that there was more to my blessing, but he felt it was too personal for the other people to hear.

In that sacred setting as the stake president and his counselor once again placed their hands on my head, I received direct, unmistakable, personal revelation.

This event has been a touchstone for me. When I begin to wonder if God knows me, sees me, hears my prayers, and loves me, I reflect back to that evening when God answered a prayer that was known only to Him and me alone.

The Good Shepherd has extended the invitation to each one of us. We can use our agency to respond or not; He will never force us. Our positive response will result in Him gathering us into the fold.

Notes

1. David A. Bednar, "If Ye Had Known Me," *Ensign*, November 2016.
2. Dieter F. Uchtdorf, "He Will Place You on His Shoulders and Carry You Home," *Ensign*, May 2016.
3. Jeffrey R. Holland, "The First Great Commandment," *Ensign*, November 2012.
4. Russell M. Nelson, "Sisters' Participation in the Gathering of Israel," *Ensign*, November 2018.

ACTIVATING THE FULL POWER OF JESUS CHRIST IN OUR LIVES

EMILY BELLE FREEMAN AND RIO GRANGE

Rio: I have come to know Jesus Christ through innumerable, small, and consistent conversations over the course of my life. Isn't that how most deep relationships are established, through a million little things?

Spending time together, some of it planned, some of it more spontaneous or unexpected. Think of someone who has seen you through the good and the bad, the joys and the sorrows, of this life. Someone you trust and feel comfortable with as you unapologetically show up in your imperfect mess because you know they're never there to judge. They see past your sweats and day-five hair, and right into your heart and where you want to be. You seek advice from them, aspire to be like them, and feel most near to your potential when you are around them. And even if time passes between conversations, they are just happy to hear from you, picking up right where you left off.

It's all of these things and more that make up a lasting, deep, and personal relationship with someone.

In short, they are with you. Every step. Every success. Every failure. Every victory. Every defeat.

Can the same be said for our relationship with our Savior?

Keep in mind, everyone's relationship with the Savior looks different, and others' relationships may be at a different stage than yours. And while it is a gift to see, watch, and hear the stories of how He shows up in the stories of others, we must not let it discourage or disappoint us because He shows up differently in our story.

It was only when we let go of what we feel it should look like, that we begin to see a relationship with our Savior unfold in a way that is personal and unique to each of us.

Emily: One of my favorite ways to read the Old and New Testament is to look for and learn from each individual's encounter with Jesus Christ. These were personal encounters, one on one. He met each person where they were, as they were, and offered His gift of grace.

The Lord appeared as a pillar of fire for Moses and clothed in armor for Joshua. He came for Peter as a lifeguard, for the soldier in Gethsemane as a healer, and for His mother as a maker of wine. He met the woman at her well, the leper in his colony, and the daughter who was dead in her very own bedroom.

He entered their stories; He showed up ready for whatever their greatest need might be—to heal the hurt, to set free the captive, to guide through the wilderness, to win the battle, to prevent from loss, to preserve from disaster, to treat carefully, to strengthen from weariness, and to make safe from danger.

These lessons remind me that the best way to understand the gift of the Savior's Atonement is to personally experience it. Consider the moment when Christ came to the Americas. "Arise and come forth unto me," He told the multitude who was in desperate need of His healing, of His grace. The ones who had been in a dark place. The ones in want, the ones falling short. "Arise and come forth unto me, that ye may thrust your hands into my side, and also that ye may feel the prints of the nails in my hands and in my feet, that ye may know, that I am the God of Israel, and the God of the whole earth, and have been slain for the sins of the world" (3 Nephi 11:14).

Feel this, He said. Touch it. Experience the sacrifice, so you will know.

When was the last time you took an opportunity to see and feel and know the grace that is offered through the Atonement of Jesus Christ?

> And it came to pass that the multitude went forth, and thrust their hands into his side, and did feel the prints of the nails in his hands and in his feet; and this they did do, going forth one by one until they had all gone forth, and did see with their eyes and did feel with their hands, and did know of a surety and did bear record, that it was he. (3 Nephi 11:15)

What does that look like for each of us?

Rio: We may never come to experience the Atonement of Jesus Christ for ourselves if we aren't aware of what might be preventing us from accessing His full redemptive powers. I want to share three limiting beliefs that I have often fallen victim to, and still do, that might be getting in between us and the fullness of the Atonement of Jesus Christ.

For those that might be unfamiliar, a limiting belief is a state of mind, conviction, or belief that we think to be true that limits us in some way. For many of us, these limiting beliefs are the stories we tell ourselves often enough that it can become very hard to change out the record playing in our minds, and we never realize the inhibiting power they have.

It can also be said that limiting beliefs are a common tool of the adversary, for he seeks to limit our understanding, hinder our growth, and prevent a deepening relationship with our Savior— all of which are the unfortunate consequences when we do not allow the voice of the Lord to prevail and instead listen to Satan's deceptive messages.

For example, one limiting belief about the Atonement of Jesus Christ might be, "Heavenly Father is tired of hearing from me about this same weakness over and over again. Surely, the Savior's Atonement does not apply this many times to the same mistake."

This short narrative played in my mind long enough, and often enough, that I began to believe it to be true. Needless to say, it has had a profound negative impact on how I approach and perceive the Savior and His sacrifice for me.

There was so much I needed to learn and relearn about the character of my Savior. This teaching from Elder Lynn G. Robbins reminded me just how limiting and untrue this belief is.

> No one is more on our side than the Savior. He allows us to take and keep retaking His exams. To become like Him will require countless second chances in our day-to-day struggles with the natural man, such as controlling appetites, learning patience and forgiveness, overcoming slothfulness, and avoiding sins of omission, just to name a few. If to err is human nature, how many failures will it take us until our nature is no longer human but divine? Thousands? More likely a million.[1]

Because of the Savior and His Atonement, how many chances am I given to turn again and become a new creature? How many chances does the Savior's Atonement provide for us to turn again (and again) and become new creatures?

"Yea, and as often as my people repent will I forgive them their trespasses against me" (Mosiah 26:30).

In other words, as many as it would take. He doesn't mind that you keep coming back to Him with the same mistake or struggle or question; He only cares that you keep coming back with "real intent" (Moroni 6:8) and a sincere desire to change. Your Father in Heaven isn't counting the mistakes. We know this to be true because He says in Doctrine and Covenants 58:42, "He who has repented of his sins, the same is forgiven, and I, the Lord, remember them no more."

But He is taking note of every time you turn again and remember His Son, He who paid the price for your transgressions so that you could pick yourself back up, try again, and be transformed, piece by piece, through His redeeming grace.

It does not serve us to stack our past mistakes and shortcomings that have already been addressed when we're faced with the same weaknesses. The Savior meets us where we are and is only worried about the next step we take. Even if we need to take the same step a few different times.

But it can be discouraging. In our limited vision on earth, our spiritual growth and progress are often imperceptible. Which is why it might feel like we are often back at the same place we were before. We must offer ourselves the same patience God offers us and remember that "an essential element of forgiveness includes forgiving ourselves."[2]

Another limiting belief we might fall victim to is, "The Atonement of Jesus Christ is only for the big sins, not my everyday weaknesses. I am expected to overcome those myself."

We might be familiar with this narrative because the Atonement of Jesus Christ is often spoken of in reference to larger sins or transgressions, where a greater process of repentance is needed.

But as of late, I have been so grateful for the reminder that His sacrifice and suffering covered much more than that. And thankfully so. Because not a day goes by that we are not faced with the ever-present truth that we are an imperfect people in a fallen world. This is not meant to be a dooming reality, but rather an invitation to return. A returning to our Maker who carefully weaved weaknesses into the very fibers of our being as a roadmap back to Him. Otherwise, why else would we need the enabling grace of an all-loving Savior?

This is where we can come to understand that the power of the Atonement of Jesus Christ is something we can activate daily. This is the process of becoming and transforming that looks like leaning on Him hour by hour as we invite His grace to make up the difference. But this can also be something we can easily forget.

Elder Bednar spoke of this limiting belief when he said:

> Most of us know that when we do wrong things, we need help to overcome the effects of sin in our lives. . . . We may mistakenly believe we must make the journey from good to better and become a saint all by ourselves, through sheer grit, willpower, and discipline, and with our obviously limited capacities. . . .
>
> The world will try to tell us it is those things alone that will enable us to be the person we hope to become. Yes, they are necessary, but they are "ultimately insufficient for us to triumphantly complete this mortal journey.[3]

So why don't we approach His enabling power with that same eagerness that we approach self-improvement books and personal development resources? Instead there is often a heaviness and shame as we approach the Savior with our desire to change and repent. It is absolutely a gift that too often goes underused. He waits to embrace you, and He longs to cheer you on, because He never expected you to do it on your own.

Which leads me to the third limiting belief: "The Savior is waiting for me to reach perfection before He will welcome me with loving arms."

This is one that I think many of us know in our hearts is far from true, yet our actions and expectations of ourselves speak otherwise.

More than thirty years ago, in the April 1989 general conference, Elder Marvin J. Ashton also saw this as a common misconception. He said, "I feel that one of the great myths we would do well to dispel is that we've come to earth to perfect ourselves, and nothing short of that will do."[4]

What finally dispelled the myth for me was when I realized the Savior wasn't just waiting for me at the end—for me to come with it all figured out, or every doubt set aside, or every bad habit broken on my own—but He was there with me at the beginning, with me in the messy middle, and with me to plead my cause when my earthly journey comes to an end.

He is not the end to our story; He is on every page, if we let Him be.

For this reason did He suffer every pain, heartache, regret, and sorrow, that He may know "know according to the flesh how to succor his people according to their infirmities" (Alma 7:12). If He were supposed to simply be there at the end to receive us, there would be no need for His succoring. He did not fight through the suffering only to watch us fight and suffer alone. God sent His Son to fight alongside us.

When we are faced with these limiting beliefs, let us call out the work of Satan and break down the barriers that are denying us the fullness of the Atonement of Jesus Christ.

In the words of Elder Ashton, "As we measure our worthiness, let us no longer put limitations upon ourselves. Rather, let us use those strengths and powers that are available to make us worthy to gain great heights in personal development."

Strength and power come from replacing the limiting narrative with God's hopeful and merciful message—"My grace is sufficient for thee: for my strength is made perfect in weakness. Most gladly therefore will I rather glory in my infirmities, that the power of Christ may rest upon me" (2 Corinthians 12:9).

Emily: These limiting beliefs remind me of the story of the widow in the treasury found in Mark 12. Jesus stood in the treasury and saw her poverty, her falling short, her want, as she faithfully put her last two mites into the same vessel that was overflowing with everyone else's wealth. He saw that, and He still allowed it to happen. He stood back and watched the widow give all that she had, even all her living (see Mark 12:44).

Because of her want.

The word *want* can be translated in Greek to mean falling short, and sometimes I swap out the word when I study these verses to read that way, "For all they did cast in of their abundance; but she of her [falling short] did cast in all that she had, even all her living" (Mark 12:44). That sense of falling short seems to describe what Rio defined for us: that process of continually trying to overcome weakness and sin and that longing to find healing in the midst of mortality. Perhaps this moment at the treasury is one each of us has experienced.

We learn the widow was not the only one who came into the treasury that day. There were others who came into that place. Perhaps they came out of habit born of culture, and tradition, and expectation. There were probably many who entered that day simply to check something off their list of things to do. The process did not grow them or strengthen their relationship with the Lord. They gave because they had, they gave of their abundance; there was no reason not to.

Contrast that with a woman who probably thought things through in great detail that morning before she left her home. This was all she had. It was all her living. I wonder if she questioned, Do I use this money for bread, or do I go hungry and give this to the Lord? Why would she choose to go hungry? And what were the thoughts running through her head as she walked to the temple that morning, as she approached the vessel overflowing with everyone else's abundance? Did her steps slow as she reached the giant vessel? Did her hand clutch those two mites desperately before they slipped through her fingers and into the great abundance there? Were her two mites really even necessary? In the big scheme of things, what difference would they make?

I can't help but wonder what the widow understood in that moment at the treasury. Perhaps want, or falling short, teaches one principle that is hard to come by in any other way.

His grace will make up the difference.

Maybe you have never thought about the cost of that one word. How grace makes up the difference of falling short, and want, and places of poverty. Grace is what you long for deep in your soul when what you are and have and qualify for is not enough.

What is the cost of grace?

We don't have the opportunity to ask the widow about her experience. We know the extent of her poverty at the treasury, but we don't know how her story ends. And maybe she represents each of us in that regard. Maybe you stand in the treasury with the choice of dropping in your two mites or going hungry. Maybe you are in a place of want, of falling short, and you wonder how your story is going to end.

I believe resilience and discipleship and exaltation are forged in the fire of falling short. I've met the Lord in the treasury. In my places of poverty. He showed up because of my want, in those moments of falling short, and offered His enabling grace.

What is the cost of grace?

The treasury exacts a cost, and I have felt the burden of that cost. I have clutched those two mites desperately. I have sacrificed all and then prayed for His grace to make up the difference.

Who pays the cost of grace?

• • •

"And Jesus sat over against the treasury, and beheld how the people cast money into the treasury: and many that were rich cast in much. And there came a certain poor widow" (Mark 12:41–42).

"And He looked up" (Luke 21:1).

Jesus. At the treasury. Willing to cast in more than they all, all that He had, even all His living. Because of His want. The purchase of your life for the cost of His. Your poverty, your falling short.

Christ's atoning sacrifice makes grace possible in each of our lives. He paid the cost of grace in order to offer us that gift.

Sometimes we think the cost of grace is all our living, but perhaps, in reality, it is all of His. He gave all His living, His life, to redeem ours. The cost of grace is sacrifice. The Father giving His Son. The Son giving His life. Each of us giving over our life as-is. It's turning our lives over to Him. All our living, our want, our poverty, our falling short, believing He will make up the difference, He will help us overcome, He will help us become, through grace.

I love understanding that falling short is not only natural but essential to our journey in mortality. I believe it is our falling short that causes us to yearn for a relationship with Jesus Christ. Perhaps that relationship is built on a million little things, every one of our moments at the treasury of sacrifice forging the relationship, each individual experience allowing Jesus Christ to become real and personal to us. In my own experience, it was my weakness, my falling short, that prompted me to reach out to Him and plead for His grace, and that is what activated the full power of Jesus Christ in my life. The gift of healing and enabling strength to help me overcome, but also the transformative power of grace to help me become the woman He knows I can be.

It is important to remember we are not alone in those moments at the treasury. He is there. The refining process was never meant to be faced on our own. Purification is a process that requires the skill of a refiner. One who knows how to perform His great work in us. The great work of grace. It is a process that is described beautifully in Isaiah 43:1–5.

> But now thus saith the Lord that created thee, . . . Fear not: for I have redeemed thee, I have called thee by thy name; thou art mine. When thou passest through the waters, I will be with thee; and through the rivers, they shall not overflow thee: when thou walkest through the fire, thou shalt not be burned; neither shall the flame kindle upon thee. For I am the Lord thy God, the Holy One of Israel, thy Savior. . . . Since thou wast precious in my sight . . . I have loved thee. . . . Fear not: for I am with thee. (Isaiah 43:1–5)

It is the process of a lifetime, a million little things, every trip to the treasury that eventually adds up to the most beautiful treasure: A personal relationship with Jesus Christ. The One who will meet us where we are as we are to offer grace. The One who enters our story, and brings healing there. The Master Refiner who knows how to perform His great work in us. The One who will be there every step of the way.

Notes

1. Lynn G. Robbins, "Until Seventy Times Seven," *Ensign*, May 2018.

2. Larry J. Echo Hawk, "Even as Christ Forgives You, So Also Do Ye," *Ensign*, May 2018.

3. David A. Bednar, "The Atonement and the Journey of Mortality," *Ensign*, May 2018.

4. Marvin J. Ashton, "On Being Worthy," *Ensign*, May 1989.

MAKING CHOICES AND MOVING FORWARD WITH FAITH IN CHRIST

RHEA MAYNES

About six years ago, my husband and I were faced with a decision many adults face: to stay or to move. We were both working, new in our careers, and he had the opportunity for a big step forward in Boston. We talked it out, weighed pros and cons, and took our decision to the Lord. From there, we continued to make many choices both individually and as a couple, some right and some clearly wrong. Every time we made a choice, we had to wonder, "Where will this lead?" In April 2019, President Dallin H. Oaks gave an address by that title. He remarked, "Our present and our future will be happier if we are always conscious of the future. As we make current decisions, we should always be asking, 'Where will this lead?'"[1]

Remaining conscious of the future can be taxing, especially when you are concerned that you might be making the wrong choice. Mounting pressure to make perfect choices can often "rob our freedom, heighten our anxiety, and lower our productivity.

. . . People who try to make the perfect decision every time tend to suffer more anxiety about their decisions, feel less satisfied with them afterward, and, unsurprisingly, are less productive."[2] Several times in my life, I have experienced the paralyzing effect of seeking the perfect choice while avoiding the wrong one. In these moments, I needed to find confidence in myself and move forward with faith in Christ.

Marriage and family therapist Carol Kim has said, "Every time you make a choice, you are stepping in the direction of knowing who you are." Not all choices are between "right and wrong." In some instances (such as what to eat and what to wear), our choices simply depend on preferences. In short, making our own choices can help us figure out who we are, which can lead to increased self-confidence. Consider the college student deciding on a major. Prior to admission, they likely have an idea of their academic strengths and interests, whether that be the sciences, liberal arts, humanities, or something else. For me, I loved the sciences and came from a family of engineers. My parents are both engineers and my older sister is also an engineer. As a result, I felt pressured to follow in their steps and started off freshman year as a chemical engineering major.

Out of interest, I took an introduction to neuroscience class. While difficult, it inspired me more than any other class and quickly became my major. Studying neuroscience challenged me, altered my career aspirations, and opened new doors.

As an added surprise, the detailed study of the nervous system and chemistry brought me closer to my Savior and strengthened my testimony. Choosing a major for myself and remaining committed to it required tremendous sacrifice but yielded self-discovery, self-confidence, and increased faith in Christ.

Part of the journey to eternal life involves exploring—exploring our likes and dislikes, our passions and talents. Exploring relationships, opportunities, and environments. When my husband and I moved to Boston, we had destination days and exploration days. Destination days were days we went to work or ran errands. We set about with a destination in mind, typically to accomplish a task. Our exploration days were mutually beneficial to making Boston our home. It is how we found new places to eat, discovered our favorite spot in the park, met neighbors, and learned our way around town. As you make both daily and life-changing choices, I encourage you to consider, "Where will this lead?" Whether you have an exact destination in mind (such as a specific career) or are setting aside time to explore, always be mindful of where it may lead you and how it will benefit you today and tomorrow.

What if a destination choice doesn't quite take us where we intended to go? What if a decision we made at work, in a calling, or as a parent is not yielding the desired results? Or why would the answer to our prayers send us down the wrong road? Elder Matthew Holland, son of Elder Jeffrey R. Holland, once shared a story of driving home from the Grand Canyon with his father.

> It was dusk, and we had only gone a bumpy mile or two when we came to a fork in the road. We stopped. Dad was not certain which trail we had come in on. He knew he had to make the right decision. There wasn't much light

left, light he desperately needed to ensure he could make the correct turns the rest of the way home.

Wasting time on a wrong road now meant we would face the difficult task of making our way home in the dark.

As we did whenever we had a family problem or concern, we prayed. After we both said amen, Dad turned and asked me what I thought we should do. I answered and said, "All during the prayer, I just kept feeling, 'Go to the left.'" Dad responded, "I had the exact same impression." This was my first experience receiving and recognizing revelation.

We started down the dirt road to the left. We had traveled only about 10 minutes when our road came to a sudden dead-end. My father promptly whipped the truck around, roared back to that fork in the path, and started down the road to the right. Fortunately, there was still just enough light to help us navigate the web of dirt roads that would take us home.

As they reflected on this experience, Mathew was confused. They had prayed but felt prompted to drive down the wrong road first. Why? His father responded,

The Lord has taught us an important lesson today. Because we were prompted to take the road to the left, we quickly discovered which one was the right one. When we turned around and got on the right road, I was able to travel along its many unfamiliar twists and turnoffs perfectly confident I was headed in the right direction. If we had started on the right road, we might have driven for 30 minutes or so, become uneasy with the unfamiliar surroundings, and been tempted to turn back. If we had done that, we would have discovered the dead-end so late that it would have been too dark to find our way back in totally unfamiliar territory.

Matthew Holland summarizes their lesson to us, stating:

> Sometimes in response to prayers, the Lord may guide us down what SEEMS to be the wrong road—or at least a road we don't understand—so, in due time, He can get us firmly and without question on the right road. Of course, He would never lead us down a path of sin, but He might lead us down a road of valuable experience.
>
> Sometimes in our journey through life we can get from point A to point C only by taking a short side road to point B. We had prayed that we could make it safely home that day, and we did.[3]

When we realize that a choice might be the "wrong road," we should adapt a new mindset.

First: You are not a failure.

Let me repeat this. *You are not a failure.* It is often by missteps that we learn some of the most valuable lessons and become better versions of ourselves. Consider how infants learn to walk. Walking requires balance, posture, strength, and motor control, all of which begin to develop from birth. First steps are usually met with falls, and even after weeks of standing and stepping, falls often occur. If our intentions are good (intentions such as loving our neighbor but our words fall short) and our choices stem from righteous desires (such as seeking an eternal marriage but it's falling apart, or caring for another and unknowingly getting them sick), if your intentions and desires are right, then you are not a failure. You are learning.

Second: You are learning.

When wrong choices manifest, it can be a win-win. You have the opportunity to course-correct while learning valuable lessons about yourself and the plan Heavenly Father has for you. You can turn around and know for a surety that the other road is the way home.

Third: You are not facing this misstep alone.

If you choose, you can take a step in the right direction as you move forward with faith in Christ. Mistakes are an antagonist to self-confidence. When you find yourself doubting in your abilities, have faith. Proverbs 3:5–6 reads, "Trust in the Lord with all thine heart; and lean not unto thine own understanding. In all thy ways acknowledge him, and he shall direct thy paths."

In the summer of 2019, my husband and I became parents. We welcomed our healthy son to this world with all of the excitement and anxiety you would expect from new parents. Since we had recently moved to a new area and didn't have family nearby, I decided to step away from my career and stay at home full-time. As weeks passed, all of the change combined with hormones darkened my world. What started out as self-defeating thoughts grew into a depression so deep that I began to think my life had no meaning. I cried to God in desperation. "If I am worthless, why am I even here? I don't have anything left to give. I want to give up." As tears soaked my face, I felt loved. I then had a perfect knowledge that my life was not meant for this moment and that this is not the whole plan God had for me. I clearly remembered that Jesus Christ suffered so that I can have joy. The love I felt turned into a type of light that lifted the darkness enough so I could have energy to get help. His love and light never left.

I wasn't joyful overnight, but when I was suffering, my faith in Christ helped me move forward. Making the choice to attend church, pray, and read the scriptures, along with having righteous desires, has brought me closer to the Savior so I could reach Him in my most desperate moments. I can testify of the truthfulness of these words by President Russell M. Nelson:

> When you reach up for the Lord's power in your life with the same intensity that a drowning person has when grasping and gasping for air, power from Jesus Christ will be yours. When the Savior knows you truly want to reach up to Him—when He can feel that the greatest desire of your heart is to draw His power into your life—you will be led by the Holy Ghost to know exactly what you should do.[4]

In order to reach Him, we must *choose* to reach out. "Knock, and it shall be opened unto you" (Matthew 7:7). The Lord does not want us to emotionally suffer. He will help us make hard decisions, provide us with strength to reach the finish line, and comfort us in corrections. When we choose to invite Christ into our journey, we'll find a strength beyond our own.

The scriptures are filled with stories of the righteous making sacrifices to serve our Father in Heaven. Christ even called some of His disciples while they were actively working in their livelihoods. They "straightway left their nets and followed him" (Matthew 4:20). As we consider the opportunities before us, what are we willing to sacrifice to reach not only our goals and righteous desires but the greatest gift God has to offer, eternal life? Are we prepared to "straightway" leave our nets and follow Him? Last year my dad was called as the mission president for the Louisiana Baton Rouge Mission. He retired a few months prior and was financially and spiritually prepared to answer the call to serve. My mother's circumstances were different. As his companion, she would need to straightway leave her net to serve. Since my mother was a teenager, she had dreamed of working for NASA. After graduating from college, she got her dream. She was a NASA employee.

I took pride in and loved seeing my mother give her all in both of her jobs: as a NASA engineer and as a mother. After about thirty years, she was in the height of her career. She oversaw part of the development of the Mars Rover project. To fulfill this role, she and my dad split their time between California and Florida. As the project wound down, she was back full-time in Florida when they got the call, and they both immediately said yes. "Yes" meant that my mom had to resign from her dream job at its height. "Yes" meant that she missed the launch of the rover by days and would miss being present for the landing. "Yes" also meant that she had developed a deep and sincere love for Christ and chose to put Him first.

Her actions have been the ultimate testimony of her faith. She made the decision to put Him first so long ago that she was going to say yes regardless of the sacrifice required. Her passion for space is nowhere near her passion for the gospel of Jesus Christ, and so many are benefitting from her sure foundation.

Where will our decisions lead? Are the decisions we make daily leading us to our desired eternal destiny? Are life-changing choices being met with faith and prayer? Are our missteps teaching us more about ourselves or strengthening our faith in Christ? Are we prepared to make sacrifices for the choices we made yesterday and move forward with faith in Christ? I hope so. "For with God nothing shall be impossible" (Luke 1:37).

Notes

1. Dallin H. Oaks, "Where Will This Lead?," *Ensign,* May 2019.
2. Dr. Margie Warrell, "Overthinking the Small Stuff? Five Ways to Make Better Decisions, Faster," https://www.forbes.com/sites/margiewarrell/2018/08/14/stop-sweating-small-decisions/?sh=7af69ed947eb.
3. Matthew Holland, "Wrong Roads and Revelation," *New Era*, July 2005.
4. Russell M. Nelson, "Drawing the Power of Jesus Christ into Our Lives," *Ensign*, May 2017.

THE PATH UNEXPECTED: MANAGING THE UNPREDICTABILITY OF LIFE

ANGELA AHN

When I was fifteen years old, my parents were in a car accident, hit by a drunk driver, while on their way to the Los Angeles temple of The Church of Jesus Christ of Latter-day Saints.

When my brothers and I arrived at the hospital, we were informed that my father had already passed away and that my mother had sustained massive traumatic injuries.

My mother ended up surviving, but her life was nothing like the life she'd had before. After the accident, she was no longer able to move, speak, eat, or drink. For the next eighteen years until her passing, she would lay in a hospital bed staring at the ceiling or propped in a wheelchair.

I don't know how my mother had the stamina to survive in this condition. I can only imagine it was her fierce concern for and love of her children that kept her tied to mortality.

In the aftermath of the accident, my brothers and I went through decades of sorrow. We faced lasting and major depression, addiction, suicidal ideation, and abuse. Our story of heartbreak and survival was long, painful, and messy—and ultimately beautifully redemptive through our Savior, Jesus Christ.

It's a story that may be similar to yours. Life is filled with challenges and opportunities that we could have never expected. What we see as "normal" life is upended in the blink of an eye. Such changes, whether planned or unplanned, can find us debilitated, exhilarated, or somewhere in between.

Embracing the unknown with faith-filled flexibility and hopeful adaptability can provide stability in an ever-changing life.

I would like to focus on three topics:

First, using our faith in Jesus Christ to override our fears.

Second, developing skills to deal with uncertainty and change.

Third, reorienting our perspectives to not simply endure a situation but to enjoy the life we have been given.

First, we can use our faith in Jesus Christ to override our fears by having a correct knowledge of and faith in Jesus Christ, *choosing* to have faith, and then taking action.

After my parents' accident, I was in a constant state of fear. Without having a correct knowledge of and true faith in Jesus Christ, my fear put me into overdrive. What looked like faith on the outside was actually a hyperactive fear I was feeling on the inside.

I became obsessed with religion—not spirituality, not true faith in Christ—but in a twisted form of religion. I thought I had done something terribly wrong to incur the displeasure of God's wrath upon me. I was certain that no amount of good works would be able to save me. Ironically, I still tried to "save myself" in order to prevent more bad things from happening, which manifested in obsessively trying to be "righteous," a condition that through therapy I later learned is called scrupulosity.

I didn't have faith in Jesus Christ and His grace, mercy, and saving power. What I was doing was having faith in ME and trying to save myself, and woefully drowning as a result.

We often talk about faith without works being dead, but the opposite is also true. Works without faith in Jesus Christ are also dead.

The first of the four principles and ordinances of the gospel is faith in the Lord Jesus Christ. This is no small statement. Although I thought I had faith in Jesus Christ, I had no idea of what this really meant.

In order for us to have true faith in God, we need to first, believe that He exists; second, have a correct idea of His character, perfections, and attributes; and third, believe that the life we are pursuing is according to His will. If we don't have these three things, then our lives are imperfect and unproductive.

I had a total misunderstanding of God's character, perfections, and attributes, and thus my life was indeed imperfect, unproductive, and very unhappy. I didn't see the Savior as a loving, merciful, and kind God. I saw Him as someone to fear. This was the first massively erroneous thought that needed to be changed.

The true doctrine to counteract my beliefs was this: "For God so loved the world, that he gave his only begotten Son, that whosoever believeth in him should not perish, but have everlasting life. For God sent not his Son into the world to condemn the world; but that the world through him might be saved" (John 3:16–17).

I had to stop believing in a punitive God and start believing in a loving God who wanted the best for me and was on my side. I had to believe in a God who loved me so deeply that He made the ultimate sacrifice for me; He suffered for my sins and gave up His life.

That is what having a true knowledge of and faith in Jesus Christ meant, but that wasn't enough. I then had to choose to have faith in Him.

Elder Neil L. Andersen said, "Faith in Jesus Christ is a gift from heaven that comes as we choose to believe and as we seek it and hold on to it. . . . Your faith is not by chance, but by choice."[1]

Choosing to have faith in Christ is not a one-time event. We need to choose Him over and over again so that when bad things happen, and our fears start to consume us, we can choose to have faith again, and cry out as the man in the scriptures did, "Lord, I believe; help thou my unbelief" (Mark 9:24).

But even having a correct knowledge of and choosing to have faith in Christ isn't enough. We must then take action. True faith moves us to action. The action we can take to deal with uncertainty and change is to build emotional resilience. As you do so, you'll be prepared emotionally and spiritually to find the stability you need in an ever-changing life.

If you are living in a current situation that you don't like, you can do something about it. If something isn't working, you can do things differently to yield different results. A loving Heavenly Father has given us the tools necessary to develop the skills to build emotional resilience, but it requires action and repeated effort.

The first skill we can develop is to have healthy thoughts. The *Emotional Resilience Manual* says, "Our thoughts are important. How we talk about ourselves and how we think about things impact how we feel and how resilient we can be. Our thoughts also play a great role in how we interact with others and perceive the world around us."

The scriptures teach, "For as he thinketh in his heart, so is he" (Proverbs 23:7).

Knowing how much power your thoughts have over your emotions, both the Savior and the adversary seek to influence your thoughts. Our thoughts lead to our emotions, our emotions lead to our actions, and our actions then create the world that we live in.

A simple yet very effective thing I do when I am stressed, ashamed, or worried is to choose to override my thoughts with positive affirmations. I repeat things like, "Heavenly Father loves you," "I love you," or "I am worth loving." Sometimes these affirmations can be scriptural, such as, "Be still, and know that I am God" (Psalm 46:10).

Sometimes, we are so deep in our unhealthy or incorrect mindsets that we're not even aware of it. I was unaware, for many years. Finding and talking with good therapists and reading therapy-based books helped me to recognize my erroneous thought processes and what I could do to change them.

If your life just isn't working and it hasn't been working for a long time, consider the possibility of therapy. For those struggling with the stigma of seeing a therapist, Elder Jeffrey R. Holland affirmed, "If things continue to be debilitating, seek the advice of reputable people with certified training, professional skills, and good values. Be honest with them about your history and your struggles. Prayerfully and responsibly consider the counsel they give and the solutions they prescribe. If you had appendicitis, God would expect you to seek a priesthood blessing and get the best medical care available. So too with emotional disorders. Our Father in Heaven expects us to use all of the marvelous gifts He has provided in this glorious dispensation."[2]

Emotional therapy is like physical therapy—it can be painful and hard at times. It also takes application and practice, but thinking and acting in different ways will yield different results. As we change our minds, we change how we feel, and when we change how we feel, we change how we act, and when we change how we act, we change our lives.

The next skill we can develop is to have a healthy body. Our bodies need regular exercise, proper nutrition, rest and sleep, and good personal hygiene. When any of these areas are off, our emotions are more at the surface and we don't have as many coping skills or solutions.

Exercise is one of the ways we can develop a healthy body, as is proper nutrition. I know that when I am eating more fruits and vegetables and taking my vitamins, I feel a lot better. I have more consistent energy throughout the day, I am more in tune with the Spirit, and I actually enjoy food more.

Other ways to manage the stresses of life are through getting adequate rest and sleep and making the time to practice good personal hygiene.

I remember marveling once at my friend as she bathed, moisturized, and brushed the teeth of her little toddler. I thought, "Wow, that child has an awesome life! How would it feel to be so pampered like that?" The irony is that she was giving her child basic care, but to me, it seemed so luxurious, because I didn't practice that level of care myself.

As women, we tend to put ourselves last, but we should realize that by taking care of ourselves, we can actually serve better.

One of the greatest blessings I have witnessed from keeping my body healthy through exercise, nutrition, rest, and personal hygiene is the ability to have the Spirit with me more strongly. This is an invaluable gift, both for myself and those I serve. President Nelson has emphasized how crucial it is that we know how to receive revelation. By keeping our bodies healthy, we become a conduit for the Holy Ghost.

The Apostle Paul taught, "Know ye not that your body is the temple of the Holy Ghost which is in you . . . ? Therefore glorify God in your body, and in your spirit, which are God's" (1 Corinthians 6:19–20).

Another skill we can develop is to have healthy relationships: with Heavenly Father, ourselves, and others. When we develop healthy relationships, we receive the support we need to help us deal with uncertainty and change.

The three types of healthy relationships I mentioned are found in the first and second great commandments, "Thou shalt love the Lord thy God with all thy heart, and with all thy soul, and with all thy mind. This is the first and great commandment. And the second is like unto it, Thou shalt love thy neighbour as thyself" (Matthew 22:37–39).

My relationship with Heavenly Father is so imperfect; however, because I lost my parents at such a young age, I had to learn to rely on Him. My daily dependence on Him includes prayer, studying the scriptures, and journaling. By recording my thoughts, feelings, and experiences, I am providing a way for Heavenly Father to communicate with me. As I do this, He provides me with ideas, knowledge, peace, and love. By studying the scriptures in this way, I am keeping a record of God's relationship with me and recognizing His hand in my life.

A friend once told me that she studies her scriptures as if she were preparing to teach a lesson. Another friend told me that he studies the scriptures and prays that he will have the opportunity to share what he has learned to bless another. These ideas have greatly influenced how I study the scriptures. Can you imagine how much this could help you as a mother, friend, colleague, or spouse?

The second type of healthy relationship we can develop is to love ourselves. We often overlook that part in the second great commandment, to love thy neighbor as *thyself*. I think we completely dismiss that part because we think loving ourselves means being selfish.

When a woman truly loves herself, she is a commandment-keeper. She respects herself and has good boundaries. A woman who truly loves herself is then more fully able to have healthy relationships with others.

Regarding relationships with others, do you know what the number one thing I've found that both married and single women struggle with? *Loneliness.*

As a single, never-married woman of forty-seven years of age, you would think that I would be lonely, but I am not. How am I not lonely?

I learned something from my parents' accident. A few years after the accident, I was nineteen years old and in college, and I started to take care of my then eleven-year-old brother. Having this responsibility to care for my younger brother gave me meaning and purpose. This kept me busy and focused on others.

I also took the opportunity to develop relationships through ministering, serving in my Church assignments, being a helpful coworker, and being a good friend.

Do you want to feel loved? Then give love. When you are the one who is acting and giving love, you are doing something about your situation.

Finally, we can reorient our perspectives to not simply endure a situation but to enjoy the life we have been given by practicing gratitude.

I used to think practicing gratitude was overly simplistic.

Then I actually practiced gratitude, and I mean, *really* practiced it, and it changed my life. I practiced gratitude by recording the things I was grateful for, by praying only in gratitude without asking for anything, and by changing my narrative.

First, I kept a daily record of the things I was grateful for. By doing so, I was tracking the ways in which Heavenly Father was blessing me, and it allowed me to feel the joy of my blessings not only once but to relive that joy again! It was humbling to see all the blessings that I would have failed to have recognized, had I not sat down and started writing.

Second, in order to reorient my perspective, I practiced intense gratitude through prayer.

Elder David A. Bednar taught a method of prayer in which the person giving the prayer would only offer thanks, without asking for anything. In the Doctrine and Covenants, we learn, "Thou shalt thank the Lord thy God in all things," which also includes our trials (Doctrine and Covenants 59:7).

I had decades of negative thinking that I needed to correct, so praying only in thanks seemed like a good way to counteract that. For example, instead of praying, "Please help me with my job. I hate my job," I would pray, "Thank you for a job that provides me with the necessities of life. Right now I am struggling, but I appreciate this opportunity to find a solution. Thank you most of all that this situation is helping me to rely more on thee."

Finally, I practiced gratitude by rewriting my narratives, or the stories I was telling myself.

We all have stories we tell ourselves, on a daily basis and at large. In telling our stories, there is always a perspective that goes along with the story we are telling. These stories are really important, for they shape our outlook on life and ultimately our destiny.

Let me demonstrate a scriptural example of different people who went through the same experiences yet had vastly different narratives. The first narrative is from Nephi, who tells his experiences as such.

"I, Nephi . . . having seen many afflictions in the course of my days, nevertheless, having been highly favored of the Lord in all my days; yea, having had a great knowledge of the goodness and the mysteries of God" (1 Nephi 1:1).

Nephi recognized he had experienced many afflictions in his life, but he also recognized the goodness of God because he had a knowledge of God.

Now I share a second narrative, as believed by Nephi's brothers, Laman and Lemuel.

> [They] . . . believing . . . that they were *wronged* in the wilderness . . . and they were also *wronged* while crossing the sea; . . . they were *wronged* while in the land of their first inheritance, . . . [they] were *wroth* . . . because they understood not the dealings of the Lord; . . . And again, they were *wroth* . . . when they had arrived in the promised land. . . . And again, they were *wroth* . . . [and] said that [Nephi had] *robbed* them. (Mosiah 10:12–16; emphasis added)

Although Nephi, Laman, and Lemuel had all gone through the same experiences, they had very different narratives. Instead of recognizing God's goodness in blessing and preserving their lives, Laman and Lemuel had chosen the perspective of constantly being wronged and robbed, and thus they were wroth. This was because instead of like Nephi, who had knowledge of the Lord, Laman and Lemuel understood not the dealings of the Lord. They were continually seeking out reasons for why they were victims.

I can relate. I thought I had been wronged and robbed, mainly by God, because I had sought my whole life to do the right things and felt I was being rewarded with one trial after the other. I thought this way for a long time until a friend told me that everyone suffers and to stop playing the victim. That's actually not what he said, but that is what I heard, and I flew into a rage, both at him and then introspectively.

My first thoughts were, "How dare he? Does he know what I have been through? What I have suffered?" and then my thoughts changed slowly and embarrassingly into "Am I really playing the victim?"

I began to write. I wrote and rewrote my narrative. I explored what could've really happened, if I could've been able to live the life that I had wanted to live.

I realized, that had I been able to pursue the life that I had wanted for myself, I most likely would've gone down some wrong paths. Or maybe I would've been just fine, but I wouldn't have gained the strength, courage, and faith that all the years of hardship had developed in me.

It was because of my parents' accident that I was forced into making critical, life-changing decisions at a young age. It was what caused me to stay true to God and shoulder the responsibility of family. I chose God and responsibility, and was furious about it for many years. However, when I decided to stop kicking and screaming and rewrite my narrative, things got infinitely better, and with surprising speed.

I've noticed that when I practice gratitude in any form, whether to God or others, more blessings seem to come my way, or at least my perspective is changed so I notice so many more blessings.

The Doctrine and Covenants say that "he who receiveth all things with thankfulness shall be made glorious; and the things of this earth shall be added unto him, even an hundred fold, yea, more" (Doctrine and Covenants 78:19).

If you have narratives that make you feel wronged, robbed, or wroth, I invite you to rewrite your narrative until you can start to recognize the hand of God in your life. Write and rewrite until you can say, as Nephi, "Having seen many afflictions in the course of my days, nevertheless, having been highly favored of the Lord in all my days . . ." (1 Nephi 1:1).

As we use our faith in Jesus Christ to override our fears, develop the skills necessary to deal with change through emotional resiliency, and reorient our perspectives with gratitude, we can not only endure, but find joy in the life we have been given. I am a living testament of that.

Notes

1. Neil L. Andersen, "Faith Is Not by Chance but by Choice," *Ensign*, November 2015.

2. Jeffrey R. Holland, "Like a Broken Vessel," *Ensign*, November 2013.

YOU MATTER TO HIM: SEEING OURSELVES IN GOD'S ETERNAL PLAN

CAROL MCCONKIE

One of the most important desires of the human soul is to feel valued, significant, and deeply loved. For each of us, the sure source of our identity, our self-worth, and our purpose is our Father in Heaven and His Son, Jesus Christ. President Dieter F. Uchtdorf taught, "God sees you not only as a mortal being on a small planet who lives for a brief season—He sees you as His child. He sees you as the being you are capable and designed to become. He wants you to know that you matter to Him."[1]

When I visit Young Women classes, I will sometimes say, "Every Sunday you stand and recite the Young Women theme, saying, 'I am a **beloved daughter** of heavenly parents, with a divine nature and eternal destiny.'" Then I ask, "How do you know?"

The answers are insightful as they talk about their families, the beauty of nature, and time spent with faithful friends and inspiring leaders. They feel their Heavenly Parents' love when they feel the Holy Ghost, live the principles of the gospel, and are true to their covenants. They see the love of God in all things that are good, virtuous, lovely, of good report and praiseworthy.[2]

Many young women have a more difficult time identifying God's love for them. They are going through the kinds of challenges that diminish the joy of young womanhood, almost extinguishing the light in their eyes and their hope for the future. Often, I ask them, "What has helped you overcome these challenges?" They share their experiences turning to God in purposeful prayer and making time for the word of God in the scriptures. Many express gratitude for the blessing of the sacrament ordinance. Some mention the spirit they feel serving others or attending the temple. They realize that their challenges have humbled them and turned them to God. Doing the seemingly small and simple things invites the Spirit of the Lord, and as they seek heavenly help, they feel that God is there, that He knows them, and that He loves them.

I testify that individually and independently, regardless of your circumstances, God is there. He knows you and He loves you. After the city of Zion was taken up into heaven, Moses records Enoch's witness "that the God of heaven looked upon the residue of the people, and he wept." Enoch must have been amazed for he asked the Lord, "How is it that thou canst weep, seeing thou art holy, and from all eternity to all eternity? . . . yea, millions of earths like this, . . . would not be a beginning to the number of thy creations." Enoch answers his own question, "and yet thou art there, and thy bosom is there; and also thou art just; thou art merciful and kind forever" (Moses 7:28–30).

Please believe that the majesty and glory of our Father's plan of happiness is for you and His love for you is boundless. You can feel God's love if you will believe four eternal truths about yourself. First, believe you are a daughter of God. Second, believe you have a Savior, Jesus Christ. Third, believe that you have a work to do. And fourth, believe you can return to Him. It is God's work and glory to offer you His greatest gifts, which are immortality and eternal life (see Moses 1:39). *It is my hope that each of you can feel and know that you have an essential place in God's eternal plan* and that you matter to Him.

Believe That You Are a Daughter of God

You are a beloved spirit daughter of Heavenly Parents, from whom you have inherited spiritual gifts and talents. You have a divine nature and destiny. Before you were born, you knew and worshipped God as your Eternal Father, and as His daughter, you accepted His plan to come to earth, obtain a body, and be created in His image, but with the imperfections that are part of mortality. Out of love for us and concern for our well-being, Heavenly Father gave commandments "that [you] should love and serve him, the only living and true God" (Doctrine and Covenants 20:19). You agreed to earthly experiences that would try you, test you, and help you learn to walk with faith in Jesus Christ and His saving power. You accepted His gift of agency and learned to make choices that would help you progress so that step by step, day by day, you could realize your divine destiny as an heir of eternal life.

Satan does not want you to understand your identity. He knows that each of you is of infinite worth and that you have a divine mission to fulfill. The prince of darkness would have you believe that your value lies in worldliness, including a focus on perfect appearance, acquiring impressive wealth, gaining recognition and the popularity of friends and neighbors with your brilliant ideas, superlative service, the number of likes on your social media posts, and, of course, your remarkable ability to successfully compete with others and gain the upper hand in every situation. He would have you believe in your own spectacular perfectionism and that if you are anything less, God has shortchanged you or that you have not lived up to God's expectations.

On the other hand, choosing to humbly worship our Heavenly Father invites the Spirit of the Lord into our hearts and minds. We know and feel that we literally are His spirit daughters and that we have inherited divine qualities and characteristics that make us who we really are.

One of my daughters has six children, and their house is a neighborhood gathering place. A little girl from up the street, who lives with her grandfather, loves coming to play. She has felt the love and comfort of a happy family there. One day the children were in the backyard playing Primary. While working in the kitchen, my daughter overheard them singing "I Am a Child of God." When the song finished, she heard this little girl's voice ask, "Do you really believe that?"

The children replied, "Yes, and you are too! We are all children of God." When their little friend heard these words, she jumped up and exclaimed, "I knew it! I just knew it!"

In her neglected little girl heart, she could feel that she is a daughter of God. She began attending Primary and eventually was baptized. She is learning her divine identity—the girl she was born to be. She is learning that we matter to God because we are His children.

Believe That You Have a Savior, Jesus Christ

In perfect love, God gave His only begotten Son to save you and me from sin and death (see John 3:16–17). The purpose of our Savior's mortal mission was to atone for your sins and for mine, to die an ignominious death, and by the power of God rise in power and glory, that you and all mankind may be raised to immortality and raised to eternal life if we will believe and obey.

Elder Jeffrey R. Holland testified of Christ's "willing submission to death [in which] He took upon Himself the sins of the world, paying an infinite price for every sorrow and sickness, every heartache and unhappiness from Adam to the end of the world. In [so doing,] He conquered both the grave physically and hell spiritually and set the human family free."[3]

Jesus Christ has set us free from sin if we repent. He also sets us free from sorrow, sickness, heartache, and unhappiness when we accept His sacred invitation to cast our burdens upon Him who is our Savior and Redeemer. By paying the price of our suffering, because He took it all upon Himself, He strengthens us to carry our burdens. The consolation of His love and His peace is upon us amid all the adversities of mortality as we look unto Him with firmness of mind. We pray with exceeding faith, and He consoles us in our afflictions. We receive the everlasting word of God and feast upon His love; "for ye may, if your minds are firm, forever" (Jacob 3:2). Our Savior calls to you and to me, "Look unto me in every thought; doubt not, fear not. Behold the wounds which pierced my side, and also the prints of the nails in my hands and feet; be faithful, keep my commandments, and ye shall inherit the kingdom of heaven" (Doctrine and Covenants 6:36–37). Out of perfect love, Jesus Christ marked the path and led the way for you because you matter to Him.

Believe That You Have a Work to Do

We need to arise to the level of our divine purposes during our time in mortality. We are here to learn the lessons that help us become like God and prepare us to return to His presence. In sacred priesthood ordinances, we made covenants that we would love the Lord and serve Him. In keeping our covenants, we access the power of God and the power to do the work God has given us to do. In keeping our covenants, we may realize all the blessings God is willing and hoping to impart.

We are here to be anxiously engaged in a good cause and bring to pass much righteousness. We learn, we work, we serve others. Whether our opportunities and experiences include a mission, marriage, a career, children or not, we choose righteousness and measure the value of our lives, with an eternal perspective.

"And the work of righteousness shall be peace; and the effect of righteousness quietness and assurance forever" (Isaiah 32:17). We withstand anything, any thought, or anyone that would diminish our divine nature or distract from our divine destiny. With humble prayer and the word of the Lord as our guide, we seek the constant companionship of the Holy Ghost. We learn and faithfully follow the Lord's will for us. When we feel inadequate, when life is unfair, when hopes and expectations are disappointed, or when blessings and burdens overwhelm us, we remember that in the strength of the Lord, we can do all things (see Alma 26:12).

Elder Holland taught:

> On those days when we feel a little out of tune, a little less than what we think we see or hear in others, . . . remember it is by divine design that not all the voices in God's choir are the same. . . . Believe in yourself, and believe in Him. Don't demean your worth or denigrate your contribution. Above all, don't abandon your role in the chorus. Why? Because you are unique; you are irreplaceable. The loss of even one voice diminishes every other singer in this great mortal choir of ours, including the loss of those who feel they are on the margins of society or the margins of the Church.[4]

We all have a work to do in God's kingdom, and everyone is needed.

A friend of mine shared an experience that, for me, is a nice parable for accomplishing the work God has given us in mortality. One day, a young father took three of his four sons on a bike ride. For Miles, the youngest of the three, it was the most challenging mountain bike ride he had yet experienced—a ride that included features such as "The Acid Drops" and "Clavicle Hill." At a particularly difficult feature, Miles watched carefully as his two older brothers stopped to survey it before successfully navigating down the path. They each chose different lines through the feature, but each line was ultimately successful.

Miles was not certain he could ride something that steep with the haphazardly placed rocks, even though he had seen his brothers do so. As he stood at the top of the hill, he said things like: "Dad, I don't want to do this." "Dad, I can't do this." But knowing the ultimate destination, it was the only way to go. So, Miles asked his father to carry his bike for him; Dad said no. He asked his father to hold onto his bike while he rode it; Dad said no. Instead, his father asked Miles to watch as he traversed down the safest line. Then, his father came back up, and told Miles to ride right behind and to follow his rear wheel closely. Miles made it safely down. He didn't have the confidence to do it alone, or after watching others show him how—but he had the confidence when he trusted and followed his father closely. And Miles felt great!

I testify that when we follow God's commands closely, He will prepare a way for us to accomplish His work (see 1 Nephi 3:7). Our Father wants us to feel healed, valued, hopeful, and successful. He gave His Son to lead the way. He gave the Holy Ghost to guide our path. He does not want us to wallow in fear, sin, self-loathing, or doubt. He wants us to feel His love, to appreciate our unique blessings and opportunities, and to live nobly, honorably, and virtuously, as a daughter of God should live. You have a work to do, and you matter to Him.

Believe You Can Return

Eternal life in the presence of God is His greatest gift to us and is reserved for those who will prepare to receive it. Those who obtain eternal life are those who pay the price to become like God in obedience, in personal righteousness, and in service to others. They have obtained the glorious promise of the Lord when He declares, "It shall come to pass that every soul who foresaketh his sins and cometh unto me, and calleth on my name, and obeyeth my voice, and keepeth my commandments, shall see my face and know that I am" (Doctrine and Covenants 93:1).

Out of perfect love, our Eternal Father offers us the continuation of the family unit in eternity and the fullness of His glory and power. King Benjamin also described this eternal condition as a state of never-ending happiness (see Mosiah 2:41). Let us walk the paths of mortality with faith in Jesus Christ, a sincere spirit of repentance, and a firm commitment to the covenants we have made in sacred priesthood ordinances. Let us prepare to receive Him at His coming, "that, when he shall appear, we shall be like him; for we shall see him as he is. And every [woman] that hath this hope in [her] purifieth [herself], even as he is pure" (1 John 3:2–3). As we ponder these truths, "Please remember . . . that the Lord blesses those who *want* to improve, who accept the need for commandments and *try* to keep them, who cherish Christlike virtues and *strive* to the best of their ability to acquire them. If you stumble in that pursuit, so does everyone; the Savior is there to help you keep going."[5]

I testify that God is our Eternal Father and we are His daughters. He loves *us* with all *His* heart, might, mind, and strength. As Elder Holland has said, God's "love is the foundation stone of eternity, and it should be the foundation stone of our daily life."[6]

Our Father loves us so much that He gave His Son to be our Savior and Redeemer. May we remember and never forget that in all things, in all places, and at all times, you matter to Him.

Notes

1. Dieter F. Uchtdorf, "You Matter to Him," *Ensign*, November 2011.
2. See Article of Faith 1:13.
3. Jeffrey R. Holland, "The Only True God and Jesus Christ Whom He Hath Sent," *Ensign*, November 2007.
4. Jeffrey R. Holland, "Songs Sung and Unsung," *Ensign*, May 2017.
5. Jeffrey R. Holland, "Tomorrow the Lord Will Do Wonders among You," *Ensign*, May 2016.
6. Jeffrey R. Holland, "Wonders among You."

BEAR WITH
MINE INFIRMITIES

AMY A. WRIGHT

Located in Leicester, England, is a typical little English country-side church. What draws people to this church from all over the world, however, is not the church itself but an inspiring inscription above the door that reads: "In the year 1653 when all things sacred were throughout this nation either demolished or profaned, Sir Robert Shirley Baronet founded this church. Whose singular praise it is to have done the best things in the worst times and hoped them in the most calamitous."

Sisters, we can do the best things in the worst times!

If we are wise and turn to the Savior, out of every tragedy, every trial, every heartache, every single disappointment comes an opportunity for priceless education and spiritual growth.

I once had an experience of doing the best things—small and simple things—in the worst times, and those things helped save my life.

October 29, 2015, was a day that began with a simple,

non-invasive surgical procedure and ended with the words, "You have cancer." And not only did I have cancer, but the original diagnosis before further testing estimated that I had about four months to live. My husband and I were stunned! As we drove home in silence trying to process the news and what this meant for our future, my concerns immediately turned to our three sons. My heart broke as I began to worry about them.

In my mind I asked Heavenly Father, "Am I going to die?" The Holy Ghost whispered, "Everything is going to be okay." Hmmm, what does that mean? So, then I asked, "Am I going to live?" Again, the answer came, "Everything is going to be okay."

I was confused. Why did I receive the same answer whether I lived or died?

Then suddenly every fiber of my being was filled with absolute peace as I was reminded that:

- We did not need to hurry home and teach our children how to pray. They already knew how to receive guidance and comfort from prayer.

- We did not need to hurry home and teach them about the scriptures. The scriptures were already familiar to them and would continue to be a major source of strength and understanding.

- We did not need to hurry home and teach them about repentance, the Resurrection, the Restoration, the plan of salvation, eternal families, the power of the Atonement of Jesus Christ—the very doctrines of salvation.

In that exact moment, every family home evening lesson, every daily early morning scripture study session, every prayer of faith offered, every blessing given, every testimony shared, every ordinance participated in, every covenant made and kept, every Sabbath day observed, even every single Church history site visited mattered—oh, how it mattered! It was too late to put oil in our lamps. We needed every single drop, and we needed it right now!

One might ask, why did I find so much comfort in these things?

Why, when staring at the prospect of our sons being raised without a mother, was the Holy Ghost whispering peace to my heart and mind?

It is because every single one of these seemingly small and simple things share the exact same foundation, Jesus Christ!

If I died, through Jesus Christ, my family would be comforted, strengthened, and one day restored. If I lived, I would have access to the greatest power on this earth to help, succor, sustain, and heal me. Because of Jesus Christ, in the end, everything will be okay.

Even so, we never know when our next trial will come. We need to be ready! Prayer, scripture study, ordinances, covenants, Sabbath day attendance . . . all these things are foundational. They form bedrock that we can securely anchor our lives to so when the winds blow and the storms rage—and they will—we will not be moved. Because of Jesus Christ and the blessings that emanate from His infinite Atonement, we can find peace, comfort, and shelter during the storms of life!

Two weeks after my third surgery, and just over a month after diagnosis, I began chemotherapy. I found myself going to the infusion room every Monday, Tuesday, and Wednesday for almost seven months. During that time, I had the opportunity to meet a lot of incredible people. My first day receiving treatment I was still very sore from surgery, scared, and nauseous. As I waited to be taken back for treatment, a man came and sat next to me and immediately started making small talk. I was grateful for his kind nature and cheerful outlook. It took my mind off the fear that was swelling up inside. The challenge was this man smelled very strongly of nicotine, which was adding to my nausea. While talking, he bent over to pick something up, and his shirt collar flapped open to revel a chemotherapy access port. I was shocked! I could not believe that he had just finished smoking a cigarette before going back into the infusion room where a team of doctors and nurses would do everything in their power to save his life!

Well, six hours later, after my first chemotherapy treatment, I was on my way home and the symptoms were already starting to kick in. I ended up spending that first night on the bathroom floor by the toilet. It felt as though every cell in my body was rejecting the chemotherapy with everything it had. By 4:00 a.m. I could not move and started sobbing as thoughts of that kind man came racing through my mind. I have never battled an addiction before. I do not know its power or what it feels like. If that dear man got even half as sick as I did while receiving chemotherapy treatments and he still could not say no to a cigarette, then what he needed from me was not my criticism but my compassion.

I learned that we come to know Christ when we withhold judgment from one another.

After surviving the first three weeks, it was time to receive another double treatment. I told my husband that I was going to quit! There was no way I am going back. This should be illegal! I am quite sure it was a human rights violation to put anyone through this kind of torture. Little did I know at the time that my treatments were just "warming up." My husband patiently listened and validated all my fears, heartache, and suffering, and then he lovingly responded, "Well, then we need to find someone to serve."

How is this possible? I am fighting for my life right now! I cannot even take care of myself! But Jesus Christ has the power to make the seemingly impossible, possible. And so, we began to serve.

As a family we organized concerts in the infusion room, knitted hats and scarves, made cozy blankets, and collected items to help relieve common symptoms. When fear of the unknown would creep in, I would distract myself by redirecting my thoughts to ways in which I could serve. Many were big; others were simple messages of encouragement and love. When the bone pain was so severe that I could not sleep, our home became an extension of the temple as I spent hours on Family Search seeking out my kindred dead.

I quickly learned that there is no such thing as a small act of kindness. Something as simple as a smile can be an answer to a prayer and help someone survive another day.

In the infusion room you tend to make a lot of friends. Friends who do not tell you what they do for a living, what kind of car they drive, where they have traveled, how much money they make, or education they have obtained. What they do is show you pictures, lots and lots of pictures, and tell you stories, lots and lots of stories about the people they love. There is never a qualifying statement or an asterisk next to their names stating, "If only they had made different choices." They simply say, "These are mine. This is who I love."

One beautiful day in March, it was time for another one of my double treatments. Our boys were on spring break and decided that they wanted to spend the day passing out "chemo kits" that they had made over the weekend for my fellow cancer patients. These kits consisted of gum, lip balm, hand sanitizer, breath mints, tissues—simple gifts that may help relieve some of the symptoms associated with chemotherapy. After passing out close to fifty kits and visiting with several patients, it was time for them to leave and make room for their cousins who were arriving shortly to sing and play their guitars. Our boys indicated that they had given away all the kits except for two. I told them that as they walked down the hall to leave, they would cross paths with people coming in and out of exam rooms and that the Lord would let them know who they should give them to. And so, they left.

A few hours later I saw the daughter of a friend of mine

walking down the hall. Her mother, a fellow cancer patient, had been struggling with her treatment. I became concerned when I realized that I had not seen this dear friend for over a month, so you can imagine how thrilled I was to see her daughter. I motioned to attract her attention and she quickly walked over for a short visit. I expressed that I had been worried about her mom and was wondering how she was doing. She started to cry and told me that they had just experienced a miracle! The night before, her mom had called to tell her that she could not receive chemotherapy treatment anymore. It was just too hard. She wondered if God knew that she existed or even cared. She decided that she was going in the following day to tell her oncologist that she was quitting. Her daughter listened lovingly and then stated that she would not be going alone. As the nurse led them down the hall the following day to an exam room, two young men approached offering gifts. My friend asked the boys, "What is this for?" One of the young men responded, "This is just to let you know that you are loved." As the boys walked away, mother and daughter looked at one another and began to cry as the Spirit confirmed that God knew she existed and that He cared. The love she felt from her Heavenly Father in that moment was just what she needed to summon enough faith and courage to continue. After hearing this story, I too started to cry as I realized that our boys had been the gift givers, instruments in the Lord's hands to remind this brave daughter of God that she is not alone and that she is loved. Dana ended up completing all her treatments and is currently in remission. Because of the simple gift of breath mints, there are now grandchildren that have yet to be born that will know their grandmother.

I learned very quickly from these service experiences that when I thought of *myself, my* situation, *my* suffering, *my* pain, the world became a very dark and dreary place. But when I turned outward and focused on others, there was light, peace, strength, courage, hope, and joy.

I learned that we come to know Christ when our focus is less about ourselves and more about others.

After months of treatment, and as my body continued to get weaker and weaker, I fought daily the desire to quit. The suffering was indescribable. One week, after spending three days in the infusion room, I collapsed on the couch, trembling and depleted. A couple of hours later I woke up to the sound of my son coming home from school. I could not move. The bone and tissue pain had set in for the week, and what I affectionately referred to as my "midweek blisters" had filled my mouth and were traveling down my throat. It was then that I realized that I had not eaten much that day and was starving. However, the thought of moving my mouth to chew or swallow was more than I could bear. As I laid motionless on the couch assessing the awfulness of my situation, I began to ask the very same questions that my dear friend Dana had asked months ago. "God, do you know that I am here? Do you even care?" Then the doorbell rang. My son went to answer it and came back holding a ninety-nine-cent, half-melted Frosty with the instructions, "Here, give this to your mom." It tasted like manna from heaven! It was the perfect consistency and melted just enough where I could swallow with little effort and yet still cold enough for it to be soothing as it went down. I could not believe it! I found out later that a dear friend who had moved to a different city a year earlier had been driving in her car when the impression came, "Take Amy a Frosty, now!" Wendy knew where that impression came from and acted immediately. I have contemplated often how she must have felt and the courage that it would have taken, knowing that on the other side of that door was a family in crisis, barely keeping their heads above the water. And her offering? A half-melted, ninety-nine-cent Frosty. Does God know that I exist? Yes! Does He care? Yes! I did not even know what I needed in that moment, but God did! How grateful I am for a dear friend who had the faith to listen to the promptings of the Spirit and the courage to act!

I learned that we come to know Christ when we have the courage to follow the promptings of the Holy Ghost.

With every trial there is a choice. We can choose to look to Christ, a Being of infinite intelligence, power, wisdom, and glory, or we can suffer alone.

I have always loved Isaiah chapter 53. Here Isaiah teaches us about the tender relationship that Christ has with God, His Father, the depth and breadth of His sacrifice, and the personal application it can have in all our lives. With prophetic insight, Isaiah describes the Atonement of Jesus Christ with these words: "Surely he hath borne our griefs, and carried our sorrows: . . . he was wounded for our transgressions, he was bruised for our iniquities: the chastisement of our peace was upon him; and *with his stripes we are healed*" (vv. 4–5; emphasis added). Through this description of the Savior's suffering, we learn that His infinite Atonement is not just for our spiritual infirmities but for our physical and emotional afflictions as well.

I have a brother that lives in Maryland. It broke his heart that he did not live close enough to help me physically while I was going through chemotherapy. So instead, he would send me pictures of his children playing, videos of them singing, or beautiful landscapes and sunsets to help lift my spirits and encourage me to go on. One of the pictures that he sent me is of Little Seneca Lake located in Germantown, Maryland.

Have you ever walked along a shoreline as the sun was either rising or setting and noticed that there seemed to be a path of light that follows you? This is exactly what my brother captured with his camera.

It is interesting to note that even though the light is evenly distributed across the entire lake, the human eye only allows us to see the path that is directly in front of us.

My question for each of you is: What is your path? What is the path that God has laid out for you?

What is it that He needs you to do and experience to help you return to Him?

The Old Testament prophet Joshua admonished the Israelites, "Sanctify yourselves: for to morrow the Lord will do wonders among you" (Joshua 3:5). The following day they crossed the Jordan on dry ground! What a beautiful reminder that what we do today determines the type of miracles we will have in our lives tomorrow.

Sisters, you are doing the best things in the worst times! Do not give up! Please do not quit! When the Savior admonished us to follow Him, that invitation was literal. He was asking us to walk as He walked, to serve as He served, to forgive as He forgave, and to love as He loved. And because that path was first tread by a God, and alone, we never have to walk alone, and there is sanctifying power in our own individual journeys.

I testify that the Atonement of Jesus Christ is the greatest power on this earth. It is the power to succor, to sustain, to edify, to enlighten, to redeem, to purify, to heal, to exalt. Because of Jesus Christ, if we are obedient and faithful, and keep our covenants to the best of our ability, repenting every day, we can become partakers of all our Heavenly Father's promised blessings—the greatest of which is eternal life and exaltation, the immeasurable blessing of returning to live with God the Father and His Son, Jesus Christ, again as eternal families and most specifically to live the type of life They live.

MY SOUL SHALL BE JOYFUL IN THE LORD

MICHELLE D. CRAIG

The following is a journal entry from a sixteen-year-old girl:

"What's the matter with me? I'm just not happy and I don't know why. I just have the emptiest feeling inside of me and I don't know what to do about it. I'm just mad at everyone and at myself. I don't feel like doing anything but I don't feel like sitting around. I wonder if I'm normal feeling this way, I wish I could understand myself."

Well, that teenage girl—forty years later—is me. What would I tell my sixteen-year-old self if I could go back to my bedroom, sit on the bed, and have a heart-to-heart talk with her? I would tell her that she is normal. I would tell her that there are times in each of our lives that are difficult. That life isn't always easy. That she will have heartaches and heartbreaks—both physical and spiritual challenges—but that she can and will find joy in every season.

In a Brigham Young University devotional in December 2018, Elder David A. Bednar said the following:

> Our gospel perspective helps us to understand that joy is more than a fleeting feeling or emotion, rather, it is a spiritual gift and a state of being and becoming. . . .
>
> Enduring joy is not a blessing reserved for a select few. Rather, every member of the Lord's restored Church who is striving to remember and honor sacred covenants and keep the commandments can receive this gift, according to God's will and timing."[1]

Here are some of the bits of advice I would give my sixteen-year-old self. These are things I have learned about experiencing this enduring joy in the middle of a life that is sometimes messy.

First bit of advice: Discover and live true to divine assignments

You have a divine nature and a loving Heavenly Father. He has given you a purpose and errand uniquely suited to *you*. Most of the time, these errands from the Lord seem pretty everyday and ordinary. As you receive them—either as gentle nudges from the Spirit, by calling, by discovery as you ponder and study your patriarchal blessing, or as you experience new personal or family roles in life—these small and simple errands combine into the Lord's greater plan for you. It is by living true to who and whose you really are—it is by coming to understand and carry out each errand to the best of your ability—that you experience joy.

In the Savior's Intercessory Prayer, He said, "I have glorified thee on the earth: I finished the work which thou gavest *me* to do" (John 17:4; emphasis added). With Christ as our example, each of us needs to find and then finish the work our Heavenly Father has given us to do—not what He has given the neighbor across the street to do. Now, there are some things that are the same for all of us. Those of us who have been baptized have made covenants to keep the commandments, to bear one another's burdens, and to "stand as witnesses of God at all times and in all things, and in all places" (Mosiah 18:8–9). But the truth is, our circumstances and the way we complete our divine assignments differ. I learn from the Savior's example that joy will be mine only when what I want is aligned with what God wants for me, not for somebody else. This is why no good will ever come from comparing. Your errand is probably different from mine. Comparing another's husband, lack of a husband, children, body, finances, accomplishments, health, or a myriad of other things will never bring joy—it will certainly not bring peace.

I do not understand why some seem to have more than their share of trials or why the Lord's timetable is different for women who have such similar desires. I have a testimony, born of personal experience, that when we are doing our imperfect best to prayerfully discover and live true to the divine assignments that we have been given, all things will work together for our good. Christ wants us to have joy here—and now. The challenge for each of us is to find joy in our individual journeys—as we have been counseled to do by prophets of God. President Thomas S. Monson said, "Find joy in the journey—now."[2]

Joy in our circumstances

President Russell M. Nelson teaches:

> Saints can be happy under every circumstance. We can feel joy even while having a bad day, a bad week, or even a bad year!
>
> My dear brothers and sisters, the joy we feel has little to do with the circumstances of our lives and everything to do with the focus of our lives.[3]

Joy in our journey comes not only as we anticipate our reunion with loving Heavenly Parents and those we have loved in life, but also when we have eyes to see and ears to hear the beauty and goodness of our everyday circumstances—even when those circumstances may be challenging. We are all familiar with the scripture in the Book of Mormon: "Men are, that they might have joy." When Lehi taught this truth he was living in the promised land—all of his riches and his comfortable lifestyle left behind in Jerusalem. Some of his children were rebelling—two of them even tried to kill him and their faithful brother. Yet still he wrote, "Men are, that they might have joy" (2 Nephi 2:25).

One might ask: How can I experience this kind of joy when things are so hard? I think it has to do with our response to the challenges.

I love the oft-repeated story of Francis Webster, a pioneer who, with his wife, Betsy, crossed the plains as members of the ill-fated Martin Handcart Company. Decades after their crossing, an old man by then, Brother Webster sat in the back corner of a Sunday School class listening to a discussion becoming increasingly sharp in its criticism of Church leaders for allowing the handcart Saints to leave so late in the season. When he could stand it no longer, he arose and said, in part:

> I ask you to stop this criticism. You are discussing a matter you know nothing about. . . . I was in that Company and my wife was in it. . . . We suffered beyond anything you can imagine, and many died of exposure and starvation, but . . . [we] came through with the absolute knowledge that God lives, for we became acquainted with Him in our extremities. . . . Was I sorry that I chose to come by hand cart? No. Neither then nor any minute of my life since. The price we paid to become acquainted with God was a privilege to pay.[4]

When you think about it, is any price too high for the blessing of "becoming acquainted" with God?

When we turn to God during these times instead of away from Him, when we use these opportunities to pray more fervently, to look to Him more diligently, we can have an increase of the Spirit. Fruits of the Spirit are "love, joy, peace, longsuffering, gentleness, goodness, [and] faith" (Galatians 5:22).

I remember sitting in Relief Society one day and looking around at the women who filled the room—some of the finest women I have ever known. I know some of their stories, but not all. I looked up and down each row and looked at each sister. I thought about how much I loved her and I thought about her challenges. I could readily identify at least one major challenge that almost each was having—if I couldn't think of one, it was just because I didn't know her story well enough. As I looked at each of my sisters in that room and felt their goodness, their light, and their strength, I marveled at the refining influence of the Spirit and what those women have become—not in spite of, but *because* of their challenges. Would we choose the trials that send us to our knees? Maybe not—but would we trade the spiritual growth and understanding of God's love that comes as a result? I heard a statement once, "Joy is not the absence of pain, but the presence of God."[5] In Alma 31:38 we read: "Yea, and he also gave them strength, that they should suffer no manner of afflictions, save it were swallowed up in the joy of Christ. Now this was according to the prayer of Alma; and this because he prayed in faith."

Look for God in the Ordinary and Simple

In 1 Peter 3:10, we are encouraged to "love life, and see good days."

I love that Peter is encouraging us to see good days, not to *have* good days! He is teaching us that those who learn to love life, who find joy in the difficult journey, are those who are intentional and go about looking for it.

The following is an incomplete list, compiled from what I have learned from scriptures, the words of living prophets, and life experience. They are things that can bring us joy and help us to "see good days." (And please don't consider this a guilt-tripping addition to an already overpacked list of things to do—but rather little packets of light—any of which might stand out from time to time with a prompting to act.)

- Welcome each day no matter how it looks.
- Make and keep sacred covenants.
- Help someone keep their covenants.
- Keep your focus on others and on God.
- Remember, you can choose your response to any situation.
- You are a child of God—nourish your Spirit.
- Live in gratitude for Jesus Christ and His sacrifice.
- Recognize blessings and the hand of the Lord in your life.
- Diligently serve.
- Listen to the Holy Ghost. Ask "what lack I yet?" and then act.
- Forgive and ask for forgiveness.
- Make time for quiet and stillness.
- Whatever you do—do it well.
- Focus on God's plan of happiness.
- Choose God.
- Nurture those around you.
- Trust God and His timing.
- Stay on the covenant path.
- Be consistent in the small and simple things that bring the Spirit into your life.
- Ignore those who try to make you ashamed for living a life of discipleship.
- Find strength in your association with other believers.

- Keep the commandments.
- Resolve to be happy regardless of what is happening, or not happening, in your life.
- Look for the good in every day.
- Count your blessings.
- Don't concentrate on what you don't have or have lost.
- Look for the blessings that have come because you haven't yet gotten what you so badly want.
- Be creative.
- Smile more.
- Care for yourself and those around you.
- Repent.
- Believe and love God.
- Focus on joy; it will bring God's power into your life.
- Focus on Christ.

A story is told of an Austrian town that was suddenly invaded by eighteen thousand men, led by Marshal André Masséna, one of Napoleon's generals. The town council had almost decided that it would be best to surrender when the old dean of the church reminded them that it was Easter. He pled with them to hold church services as they usually did and to trust God with their problem. Well, they did. The French heard the church bells joyfully ringing and thought that the Austrian army had come in defense of their countrymen. Before those church bells had stopped ringing, the French army had fled.

Who would have thought that a war could be ended by the simple ringing of church bells? We have each probably known someone who, in the face of trial and suffering, has been able to ring even a small bell of joy and faith. As we try to muster our courage and find joy in covenant making and covenant keeping, as we rely on the Savior and His enabling power, we too can come off conqueror. Faith in our Savior Jesus Christ and the joy that accompanies that testimony will overcome the enemy of our souls who wants to keep us captive. It is our reaction to what we experience—the good and the bad—that will determine how our life story plays out.

I have a testimony that the glorious end of our covenant path will more than compensate for the adversity we face while on that path. In this life, and in the next, I believe that the Lord will pour out blessings upon us that will more than make up for every pain, every heartache, and every sacrifice that we are asked to make. He is a generous and a loving Father, and His timetable is not ours.

Let our hearts and souls echo the words found in Psalms, "And my soul shall be joyful in the Lord" (Psalm 35:9). As in all things, the Lord Jesus Christ is our perfect example. We are taught in Hebrews 12:2 that Christ "who for the joy that was set before him endured the cross." In speaking of this verse, President Nelson said, "Think of that! In order for Him to endure the most excruciating experience ever endured on earth, our Savior focused on *joy*!"[6]

It is my prayer that each of us can keep our focus on the joy that is set before us, on the joy that is found in our testimonies of God the Father and His Son, Jesus Christ. It is my prayer that we can come to understand who They really are and who we really are and then act accordingly.

Notes

1. David A. Bednar, "'That They Might Have Joy,'" BYU devotional, December 4, 2018.
2. Thomas S. Monson, "Finding Joy in the Journey," *Ensign*, November 2008.
3. Russell M. Nelson, "Joy and Spiritual Survival," *Ensign*, November 2016.
4. William R. Palmer, "Francis Webster," typescript of a radio address broadcast by KSUB (Cedar City, Utah), April 25, 1943, 1–2, William R. Palmer Collection, Church Archives, The Church of Jesus Christ of Latter-day Saints; William R. Palmer, "Francis Webster," *Instructor* 79 (May 1944): 217–18; David O. McKay, "Pioneer Women," *Relief Society Magazine* 35 (January 1948): 8, cited by Chad M. Orton, "Francis Webster: The Unique Story of One Handcart Pioneer's Faith and Sacrifice," *BYU Studies* 45, no. 2 (2006): 117.
5. See Darla Isackson, "Joy Is Not the Absence of Pain," in "Line upon Line" (blog), *Latter-day Saint Magazine*; https://latterdaysaintmag.com /article-1-6000/.
6. Russell M. Nelson, "Joy and Spiritual Survival," *Ensign*, November 2016.

BY SMALL AND SIMPLE THINGS ARE GREAT THINGS BROUGHT TO PASS

KATHY CHRISTOFFERSON

Several years ago, Elder Christofferson and I had the privilege of visiting the Panama Canal. Not only did we see the canal, but we got to visit the command center where the doors of the locks were controlled. Accessing that command center required us to walk across the narrow top edge of one set of closed doors of one of the locks by holding on to thin ropes on each side that served as railings. The lock on the left was full of water, only about four feet beneath us, but the water in the lock on the right was at its lowest level—a drop of seven stories! We kept our eyes on the left side.

At the command center we learned how the canal functioned. A series of locks brings a ship, in stair-step fashion, from the Pacific Ocean into a central lake at a higher elevation. The ship would then cross the lake to a second set of locks. These locks would move the ship down to the Atlantic Ocean. The process, of course, would be reversed for ships moving from the Atlantic to the Pacific.

What we found interesting was that there is no pumping of water into or out of these massive locks to raise or lower the water level. Water flows down through the locks on either side from the central lake by gravity. This works because there is an ample and constant flow of water into the lake from the surrounding rainforest. The climate is ideal for providing the quantity of water that the canal needs to function.

We thought it was stunning that massive cargo ships weighing 120,000 tons, or cruise ships eleven stories high with over 3,000 passengers plus crew, could move through this canal because of tiny raindrops that come together to form tiny rivulets, then streams, then rivers to fill the lake *and* provide for that necessary constant flow of water.

Now let me shift gears and share another experience I once had. I was sitting in a testimony meeting. As we often do, I was thinking about what I might say if I were to bear my testimony. Usually when people stand up, they have something special to say, some faith-promoting experience that happened in the past week or month. But I must admit nothing like that came to mind. I couldn't think of anything particularly remarkable.

The irony is, I do have a strong testimony of Jesus Christ and the Restoration of His true Church in these latter days. But in reflecting on the past, I realized that my testimony didn't come with one stunning event or miracle. It came by small whisperings of the Spirit. It came line upon line and precept upon precept as I heeded the words of modern prophets, studied the scriptures, followed worthy examples, and tried to apply gospel principles in my life. I haven't been perfect in these endeavors, but I have seen the hand of the Lord in my life and count that a great blessing.

When I think of these two very different events—visiting the Panama Canal and attending that testimony meeting—I am reminded of the scripture Alma 37:6, which says, "By small and simple things are great things brought to pass." While it is incredible that small drops of rain can move gigantic ships through the Panama Canal, it is even more incredible that we can receive a constant flow of spiritual impressions, even outpourings, from a Heavenly Father who is ever mindful of us. I have found that it isn't in great miracles that a testimony is kept vibrant, but in the small day-to-day affirmations and directions we receive from heaven as we strive to come unto our Savior, keep His commandments, and "be about [our] Father's business" (Luke 2:49).

Small and simple things are found in doing the basics, such as praying and studying the scriptures and acting in faith upon the promptings we receive from the Holy Ghost. These have always been stressed as actions that bring spiritual growth. Maybe just looking at them a little differently will help that growth even more. When we pray, can we accept no as an answer? Usually, we will find out in time that the Lord had helped us grow more with that "no" than the "yes" we sought.

We show gratitude to our Father in Heaven when we actually note in writing those blessings we have received. President Henry B. Eyring told of a habit he had made of jotting down a few lines each day after pondering this question: "Have I seen the hand of God reaching out to touch us or our children or our family today?" He said:

> As I kept at it, something began to happen. As I would cast my mind over the day, I would see evidence of what God had done for one of us that I had not recognized in the busy moments of the day. As that happened, and it happened often, I realized that trying to remember had allowed God to show me what He had done.
>
> More than gratitude began to grow in my heart. Testimony grew. I became ever more certain that our Heavenly Father hears and answers prayers. I felt more gratitude for the softening and refining that come because of the Atonement of the Savior Jesus Christ. And I grew more confident that the Holy Ghost can bring all things to our remembrance—even things we did not notice or pay attention to when they happened.[1]

Another thought on prayer: when we pray, do we have the courage to ask the Lord, "What lack I yet?" (Matthew 19:20). We may think the Savior would be rolling His eyes and saying, "Oh, where do I begin? The list is so long!" We've read that question being put to the Savior by a rich young man. He was told, "Go and sell that thou hast, . . . and come and follow me" (v. 21). Now, I doubt the Savior will answer you with such a tall order. But I'm sure His answer will be suited to our abilities. It could be something like, "Write a note of encouragement to Sister so-and-so," or "Try to say more positive things than negative things," or "Turn off that TV show. It will allow the Spirit to return to your home." Prompt obedience to such impressions is such a small thing, but it will bring increased ability to hear and follow further promptings from the Holy Ghost.

In getting closer to our Savior Jesus Christ, studying the scriptures—especially the Book of Mormon—goes hand in hand with prayer. I was inspired by President Russell M. Nelson's challenge in the 2018 women's session of general conference, when he asked us to read the entire Book of Mormon before the end of the year. He not only gave that challenge but also added that we should mark each reference to Jesus Christ.[2] My daughter, daughters-in-law, and I set out to do just that, and we set up a group text to encourage each other and share things we had learned.

After more than a month into our reading program, my daughter Brynn texted this: "I haven't had any real insight recently, but I just have to say that my week has gone so much better than I would have expected because I was doing my reading." When I thought about what she said, I had to admit the very same thing had happened to me. I had had a tough week with lots of pressure and demands on my time and energy, but somehow I just felt at peace all the time. To me those daily study periods in the Book of Mormon were the spiritual raindrops I needed to help me put things in perspective and keep me focused on the things that matter. I've read the Book of Mormon several times, but when I finished reading the Book of Mormon that time, I found how much richer my relationship with our Savior had become by focusing on Him. Those raindrops had formed a pool of spiritual strength that I will forever cherish. President Russell M. Nelson said this:

> When I think of the Book of Mormon, I think of the word *power*. The truths of the Book of Mormon have the *power* to heal, comfort, restore, succor, strengthen, console, and cheer our souls. . . . I promise that as you prayerfully study the Book of Mormon *every day*, you will make better decisions—*every day*. I promise that as you ponder what you study, the windows of heaven will open, and you will receive answers to your own questions and direction for your own life.[3]

I add my own witness that these things are indeed true.

One faithful member taught me how faithfulness in one seemingly small thing could change lives. Geniel Young, mother of six children, became divorced after twenty-six years of marriage and was now the sole breadwinner, with little or no support for her family. She got a job in a secretarial pool in a large Detroit, Michigan, hospital, but her family still struggled financially. For instance, when their water heater gave out, for six months they had to boil water on the stove to take baths because there was no money to fix the water heater.

Her son, Brent, recalled: "One vivid memory I have is my mother often crying in prayer behind her closed door. At one point, when our circumstances became especially constrained, she prayed more earnestly for answers and guidance. I know that she continued to pay tithing and offerings before other bills were paid. I am not sure what she paid in offerings, but it could not have been much. Around this time, there was an article in the *Ensign* [by Elder Henry D. Taylor] that had the following counsel regarding offerings: 'We can, we ought, and we must do better. . . . *If we will double our fast offerings we shall increase our prosperity, both spiritually and temporally.* This the Lord has promised.'

"She stared at the article, not knowing how she could possibly pay more," Brent said, "but she felt like she asked the question and was reading the answer meant just for her. So, she followed the counsel and doubled her offering." Almost immediately the following things happened: a plumbing problem developed, the front porch's storm door blew off in the strong Michigan winter wind, the vacuum cleaner broke, the car needed a new transmission, the furnace gave out and needed a new motor, one child chipped a tooth requiring a visit to the dentist, another child broke his glasses, and one child accidentally broke a neighbor's basement window.

With all this, Sister Young continued to pray but felt an even greater sense of desperation. She felt she had no choice but to find another job. So she put together a résumé and went to her boss and asked for a couple of personal days off work. He pressed her to know why. Reluctantly, she told him of her situation and that she couldn't live on what she was making and needed to find a higher-paying job. He was understanding and asked her to give him a little time, but he did not give her the time off. Within a couple of days, he came back and handed her a check for $2,000 and gave her a permanent raise by that amount. This was in 1974, and that amount would be equivalent to $11,000 today.

Six months later another position opened, and she was encouraged to apply. She did and got the position of administrative assistant for the hospital's chief of staff. This position came with a substantial raise. That additional income was life-changing for the family.

I was impressed by Sister Young's determination to follow the promptings of the Spirit. But more than this, I was impressed with her unshaken faith even when everything went wrong after doing the very thing she knew the Lord wanted her to do. Like handcart pioneers of old, she just kept going forward anyway, one step at a time. In humility she submitted herself to the Lord's timetable, and eventually darkness did turn to light.

I know that as we strive to stay consistently faithful even in small things, they will flow together to strengthen us spiritually in remarkable ways. As we look back, we will indeed see the hand of the Lord reaching down to bless us in a constant and marvelous manner.

Notes

1. See Henry B. Eyring, "O Remember, Remember," *Ensign*, November 2007.
2. See Russell M. Nelson, "Sisters' Participation in the Gathering of Israel," *Ensign,* November 2018.
3. Russell M. Nelson, "The Book of Mormon: What Would Your Life Be Like without It?" *Ensign,* November 2017.

I DID THIS FOR YOU

SUSAN PORTER

One Friday in February, I turned on my computer at home to join a devotional broadcast via Zoom. The speaker was Elder Walter F. Gonzalez of the Seventy. He spoke about President Russell M. Nelson's invitation to "make a list of what the Lord has promised He will do for covenant Israel."[1] Elder Gonzalez invited those listening to the devotional to share scriptures they had pondered and promised blessings they had received as members of covenant Israel.

As several people shared their thoughts, I was unexpectedly filled with the vivid memory of an experience I'd had in December 2016 when my husband and I were living in Moscow. Bruce was serving in the Area Presidency, and we rejoiced in the opportunity to meet with and learn from members and missionaries as we traveled throughout the Europe East Area.

One morning Bruce woke up and felt short of breath, so we traveled to the hospital to get a chest X-ray. It was determined that he had pneumonia and would need to stay for a few days to receive antibiotics. I went home that evening to pack up some belongings that he would need for his short stay. The next morning when I arrived at the hospital, Elder Taylor, our area medical advisor, stopped me in the lobby. He had just learned that during the night my husband's health had taken a dramatic turn for the worse, and that he had been placed in an induced coma.

In that moment, everything changed. No longer was this a routine hospital stay but a fight for Bruce's life, over five thousand miles away from family. Friends and family offered support and fasted and prayed for us. Preparations began to be put in place so that we could return to the United States to receive further medical care.

For the next twelve days I got up each morning, pleading for the Lord's help as I drove to the metro station, rode for forty-five minutes on the subway, and then walked the remaining blocks to the hospital. I sat all day by Bruce's side in the ICU as he lay perfectly still, unable to talk or move, surrounded by monitors of all kinds. Each evening I reversed my trip, arriving home to gather our belongings in preparation for our move back to Utah.

During the devotional on February 5, the Lord brought that experience clearly to my mind, reminding me that all through those cold, dark days, I never felt afraid as I traveled on the subway, standing out clearly as a foreigner. I remembered the peace and calm I felt as I sat by Bruce's bed in the hospital, and then later at home, I was alone, but not lonely, each night.

As I was wrapped in those memories, the Lord spoke clearly to my mind, "I did this for you."

Tears flowed, and I was filled with gratitude for His loving care during a traumatic time.

In that moment, the Lord let me know in a gentle and loving way that the peace I had felt, the safety I had experienced, and the sense that I was not alone had nothing to do with me and everything to do with a loving Heavenly Father and His Son being on my right hand and on my left, with Their Spirit in my heart, and angels bearing me up (see Doctrine and Covenants 84:88).

The impression was so strong that I knew there was a reason I would need this reminder of His power in my life.

Nine days after this impression, I was sitting in Elder Quentin L. Cook's office when he extended the call to me to serve as a counselor in the Primary General Presidency. I felt overwhelmed by the call. I was also filled with deep gratitude to my Heavenly Father for the knowledge He had given me that He had been with me in the past and I could rely on Him in the future.

Since that day, I have been reflecting on the clear impression I received, "I did this for you." Sisters, many of you have had traumatic experiences when everything in your life changed in a moment. Some have had trials that have lasted for years. When sorrow and tragedy come to us, we fall to our knees pleading for help. Sometimes our circumstances do not change. Sometimes it is a challenge to see the Lord's hand in our lives. Sometimes we are aware of that help, and other times we just soldier on, not realizing that it is by His power that we have the strength to carry on.

During those times, I bear my witness that God, our Heavenly Father, is with us. Even when we can't feel His presence, He is there.

One of the great blessings our Savior promised to covenant Israel, is "I will not leave you comfortless: I will come to you" (John 14:18). Whether we feel that comfort at the time or only recognize His help later, I bear witness that He will come and He will give us comfort and strength in time of need.

As I reflect on the greatest act of lifting burdens and carrying sorrows—our Savior's suffering in the Garden of Gethsemane, on the cross, and triumphant rise from the tomb—I can hear His loving words to me, "I did this for you."

I bear witness that He did it all for us.

Notes

1. "Let God Prevail," *Liahona*, November 2021.

HIS PROMISES
ARE SURE

SHERI DEW

My dear sisters, what a time we've had! Recent years have taxed every one of us in very personal ways. We were just days into a pandemic lockdown when a major earthquake hit Salt Lake City, followed by a series of aftershocks that went on for days.

Frankly, dealing with the pandemic, an earthquake, and suddenly working isolated from home rattled me. Inventorying my food storage *alone*, and scavenging among empty grocery shelves *alone*, and then being alone when my house began to shake was unnerving. During the earthquake, my brain managed to race and freeze all at the same time. There was no one to say, "You grab this and I'll grab that." No one to just dive under the table with. It was scary. One thing I've been reminded of this year is how much we need each other.

Then, three months into the pandemic, my mother passed away. Her mind had been fading, so she hadn't been herself for a while. Her passing left an immense void. A friend said to me,

"There is never a good time to lose a mother." But losing Mom during the isolation of a pandemic felt like the last emotional straw.

There is a special irony in all of this. On March 12 of 2020, I spoke at the Church History symposium at BYU. That symposium focused on the Prophet Joseph Smith, and as I prepared that message, I had the recurring impression that I should focus on what he revealed that helps us deal with loneliness. At first, I resisted the topic, but the impressions kept coming. So my topic that day was: Joseph Smith and the Problem of Loneliness.

The *moment* I sat down after delivering that message, I learned that the First Presidency had just announced they were suspending Sunday meetings. Then temples closed, and the world locked down. I thought I knew something about loneliness before March 12, 2020, but I was about to get the biggest dose of it of my life.

And the pandemic hasn't been our only challenge. Political conflict, racial tension, and economic struggles have affected many of us. Mercifully, we are not left to deal with such latter-day dilemmas alone. Peter declared that the Savior has given us "exceeding great and precious promises" (2 Peter 1:4)—which begs the question: What are those promises?

God's promises to us begin with those of the Abrahamic Covenant, to which all who accept and follow God's plan are heirs. These promises include the right to truth, priesthood, eternal posterity, and exaltation.

The promise of exaltation exceeds any other. In his first message as President of the Church, President Russell M. Nelson underscored this truth by challenging us to "begin with the end in mind."[1] He asked us to set our sights on eternity, because there is no "gift greater than the gift of salvation" (Doctrine and Covenants 6:13). But the promises don't stop there. In fact, the scriptures are *filled* with divine promises that make eternal life possible.

There is the promise of divine guidance for "feast[ing] upon the words of Christ" (2 Nephi 32:3). The promise of forgiveness for those who forsake their sins and forgive others (see Doctrine and Covenants 58:42–43). The promise of having the windows of heaven opened for paying a faithful tithe, and of eternal posterity for keeping sacred temple covenants (see Malachi 3:10; Doctrine and Covenants 132:19). The promise of having the Holy Ghost as a constant companion when virtue garnishes our thoughts (see Doctrine and Covenants 121:45–46). The promise of "great treasures of knowledge" for living the Word of Wisdom (Doctrine and Covenants 89:19). And I'm just getting started.

Let's focus on promises that can help us *right now*—promises that help us meet the rigors of the Last Days. Consider the promises associated with four gifts:

- Our divine identity
- Restoration of the priesthood
- Latter-day prophets
- The Atonement of Jesus Christ

First, the gift of divine identity. The Apostle Paul articulated the promise that comes with knowing who we are: "We are the children of God: And if children, then heirs; heirs of God, and joint-heirs with Christ" (Romans 8:16–17).

Invariably, when President Russell M. Nelson is asked questions such as how to help someone overcome addiction or how to help a struggling youth, his answer is the same: "Teach them their identity and their purpose."[2] His answer is simple but profound, because the way we see ourselves affects everything we do. So what *do* we know about who we are?

First and foremost, God really is our Father—the Father of our spirits—and we have the potential of becoming like our Heavenly Parents. But for those of us born in this dispensation, there is even more to understand about the elect nature of who we are.

In President Joseph F. Smith's vision of the redemption of the dead, he was allowed to see "choice spirits who were reserved to come forth in the fulness of times." These spirits were described as the "noble and great ones who were chosen in the beginning" to take part in this final gathering.[3]

Elder Bruce R. McConkie added that "a *host* of mighty men and equally glorious women comprised that group of the 'noble and great ones.'"[4] Sisters, these prophets, seers, and revelators were talking about us. So who are we? We are the children God reserved for the most raucous but decisive time in the history of the earth.

This is who we are. Who we have always been.

Further, because of our premortal spiritual valor, we were given the opportunity to make sacred covenants here. Through these covenants, we become heirs of all the blessings promised to the house of Israel.

Now, I'm sure there are plenty of days when none of us feel all that noble or great. But do you think there is any chance our Father would have taken a chance on the outcome of the Last Days by sending women He could not count on? There is no chance He would have done that. Our Heavenly Father did not elect us for this era only to watch us fail. We are here now because He chose us to come now.

If you've never experienced a spiritual confirmation of who you are, or if you could use a reminder, I invite you to study Doctrine and Covenants 138 and Abraham 3. Then ask our Heavenly Father if you are one of the noble and great ones. His answer will change and guide your life.

Second, the gift of the restoration of the priesthood.

For all of the positive things our world has to offer, recognizing truth is complicated. Society has become increasingly polarized in a storyline as old as Cain and Abel. Through the ages, the thirst for power, prosperity, and popularity has repeatedly led to so much contention that even faithful people have separated themselves into tribes. And history appears to be repeating itself. The Nephites and Lamanites have given way to mask-ites and anti-mask-ites; vaccine-ites and anti-vaxers; capitalists, socialists, and populists; and so on. Separating ourselves into tribes plays perfectly into Satan's hands, because disunity leaves everyone more vulnerable to deception.

Social media inflames *all* of these divisions by dishing up snippets of facts that rarely represent the *whole* truth and by providing a forum for one of Satan's most insidious tactics: flattery.

How diabolical is flattery? Look at any anti-Christ in the Book of Mormon, or anyone seeking followers for themselves. They are always masters of flattery. Sherem is a classic example: "He had a perfect knowledge of the language of the people; wherefore, he could use much flattery, and much power of speech, according to the power of the devil" (Jacob 7:4).

Flattery is telling people what they want to hear, and it is designed for one purpose: to get followers for yourself. The old adage that "flattery will get you anywhere" is why some leaders make empty promises they have no intention of keeping.

One of the greatest dangers today is that few know where or how to find truth. Many don't believe in absolute truth at all. They don't believe there is such a thing as right and wrong. But as President Dallin H. Oaks declared, "Some things are simply, seriously, and everlastingly wrong."[5] Likewise, some things are eternally true, regardless of how many polls or pundits declare otherwise. This sobering state of affairs is one reason the promises associated with the restoration of the priesthood are so precious.

What promises do we have because the priesthood has been restored? There are so many that it's hard to know where to begin.

We have the privilege of receiving revelation, of having the "heavens opened" and *always* having the Spirit with us (see Moroni 4:3), of "receiving the mysteries of the kingdom of heaven," and of enjoying the "communion and presence of God the Father, and Jesus [Christ]" (Doctrine and Covenants 107:19).

We can experience the ministering of angels and partake of ordinances that gives us access to "power of godliness" (Doctrine and Covenants 84:20). And then there is the promise repeated more often in scripture than any other: "Ask, and it shall be given you; seek, and ye shall find; knock, and it shall be opened unto you" (Matthew 7:7).

The implications of that promise are stunning. Yes, we live in complex times, but as Elder Gary E. Stevenson said, "The Restoration of the gospel of Jesus Christ offsets *perilous* times with the *fulness* of times."[6] We have *more* access to *more* power and *more* knowledge than any people anytime. This is the dispensation when "nothing shall be withheld" from the faithful (Doctrine and Covenants 121:28). We have not been left alone to wander in the dark. For "the Spirit speaketh the truth and lieth not. Wherefore, it speaketh of things as they *really* are, and of things as they *really* will be" (Jacob 4:13; emphasis added).

No wonder President Russell M. Nelson warned that "it will not be possible to survive spiritually without the guiding, directing, comforting, and constant influence of the Holy Ghost." Which is no doubt why he pled with us to "increase [our] spiritual capacity to receive revelation."[7]

This is crucial, because no one is a better liar than Satan. He too makes promises, but the *only one* he will keep is his pledge to make us as despicably miserable and enslaved as he is.

The best way to detect the adversary's deceptions is to rely on the Holy Ghost, which speaks to both our minds and hearts. He communicates both ways because you cannot convince your mind of something your heart does not feel. The Holy Ghost *is* the antidote to flattery.

Our temple covenants enhance our ability to open the heavens. President Russell M. Nelson declared that "the heavens are just as open to women who are endowed with God's power flowing from their priesthood covenants as they are to men who bear the priesthood."[8] Increasing our capacity to receive revelation is inextricably linked to temple ordinances and their power.

Receiving revelation is vital for those wrestling with questions and doubts about the gospel. Be careful not to confuse the two. If the Spirit has borne witness to you that Jesus is the Christ, Joseph Smith was a prophet, the Book of Mormon is the word of God, and President Nelson is a living prophet, then you have a testimony—regardless of any questions you have. I have plenty of unanswered questions and too many areas of gospel study where my knowledge is too thin. But these realities don't negate the many witnesses I've received of the Savior and His gospel. Sincere questions are opportunities to seek truth, not threats to testimony.

We don't have to wonder what is true. We don't have to stew over unresolved questions. We can ask those questions of our Father in Heaven and expect His help. Inspired questions lead to spiritual growth.

If we want to have access to the power of God, we have to go where His power is. His power lies in His priesthood, which is why covenant keepers have more access to His power. Perfection is not required, but covenant-keeping is. Repentance makes covenant-keeping possible. It allows us to start again and again, and to thus access the power of God.

If you aren't sure how to receive revelation, ask Heavenly Father to teach you what it feels like *for you* when He speaks to you through the Holy Ghost. Note the scriptures you are led to and impressions about things that will invite the Spirit more abundantly—perhaps media to eliminate, a grievance to resolve, ways to make your prayers more effective. If you want to learn the language of revelation, the Spirit will teach you. Every spiritual privilege is available to us because the priesthood has been restored.

Third, the gift of prophets.

The Lord *makes* and *fulfills* promises through His prophets, for "whether by [His] own voice or by the voice of [His] servants, it is the same" (Doctrine and Covenants 1:37–38).

The sobering truth, however, is that throughout history, most of the people, most of the time, have not believed in prophets. Today, a relative few believe that the Lord has *again* sent *many* prophets to the earth. Many find the words of our fifteen prophets, seers, and revelators inconvenient and politically incorrect. But prophets are under covenant to teach truth. They don't stoop to flattery, which is why they may seem unbending—especially with moral relativists who play to the crowd and deny the existence of absolute truth.

Those who choose pundits over prophets make the tragic choice of being led by "foolish and blind guides" rather than *seers,* whose ordination allows them to see things we don't see and to detect spiritual subterfuge before the rest of us can (Helaman 13:29). Prophets are one of God's greatest gifts to His children. They form an unfailing safety net of truth.

I recently witnessed our prophet giving a unique kind of inspired direction. On September 17, 2020, I was invited to attend a Zoom meeting with President Nelson, Elder Ronald A. Rasband, and Michael Colemere, the managing director of Church Communications.

Among other things, we discussed the possibility of President Nelson recording a message of hope for members. He told us to "sprinkle a little fertilizer" on that idea and bring it back to him the following week.

But then, the very next day, President Nelson asked to meet with us again. He told us our idea wasn't bad; it just wasn't right. During the night he had received direction that he did indeed need to record a message—but for the world, not just for Church members. The message was to be about expressing gratitude to God and should include a prayer for the world. He told us the day and time the video should be released and even how long his message should be.

As he spoke, I knew that I was having the rare privilege of witnessing a prophet act on revelation he had received.

We were assigned to assemble a team of videographers, translators, and other communications experts to fulfill President Nelson's instructions. If this talented group had resorted to their own expertise, they would have never recommended a video as long as the one President Nelson specified. Nor would they have suggested releasing it on a Friday.

But we had heard a prophet speak, and everyone went to work. The result was the #GiveThanks video released on November 20, 2020. And the results? Unprecedented. That video's reach through social media and on television networks in various countries dwarfed anything the Church had ever released, especially to those not of our faith. Never before had so many people heard a prophet's voice. And why? Because we heeded the counsel of a seer, who could see things we could not.

Some people get tangled up in the question, "Are prophets, seers, and revelators infallible?" That's the wrong question. A better one is, *Who exactly are* prophets? They are the ordained holders of priesthood keys that authorize the Lord's power to be distributed throughout the earth. They may not be perfect. They are, after all, still human. But they are the most inspired leaders on earth, and their only motive is perfectly pure—to help us find our way back home by pointing us to Jesus Christ.

The Lord has promised that if we receive the prophet's words as if He spoke them, the gates of hell will not prevail against us and the Lord will disperse the powers of darkness and cause heaven to shake for our good.

Accepting the gift of a prophet and following His counsel unleashes a score of promises to help us deal with the turmoil of the last days.

Fourth, the gift of the Atonement of Jesus Christ.

The Lord has declared that in the end of times, "the saints

shall . . . receive their inheritance and be made equal with [the Lord]" (Doctrine and Covenants 88:107). My feeble mind can't comprehend how *we* can be made equal with Jesus Christ. But suffice it to say, that when the Savior atoned for us, He made every good thing, *every spiritual promise*, possible.

Because of Him, we don't have to face the world and the adversary alone, don't have to bear the weight of our sins ourselves, don't have to deal with weakness, sadness, mistakes, or disappointment alone.

Helaman described what Jesus Christ promised to all who build their lives upon the foundation of His gospel: "When the devil shall send forth his mighty winds, yea, his shafts in the whirlwind, yea, when all his hail and his mighty storm shall beat upon you, *it shall have no power over you* to drag you down to the gulf of misery and endless wo, because of the rock upon which ye are built, which is a *sure foundation*, a foundation whereon if men build they *cannot fall*" (Helaman 5:12; emphasis added).

What an incredible promise! That if we will just build our lives on Christ, Satan *cannot* drag us down and we *cannot* fall.

Most of the Lord's promises *are* conditional. He is bound when we do what He says, but when we don't, we "have no promise" (Doctrine and Covenants 82:10). So *we* are the ones who decide if we will do what is required to receive His promises. And we are the ones who decide if we will continue to believe, even when some promises don't materialize as we hope.

I've learned in a poignant way that the Lord has His own timetable. He fulfills some promises quickly and some over long periods of time. But that does not mean He isn't blessing us throughout the process.

For more than four decades, I have prayed, fasted, and pleaded for an eternal companion. When I was called to the Relief Society General Presidency at age forty-three, I would have never believed I would still be unmarried at this age. To this day, I don't understand it. Let me simply say that I am well acquainted with disappointment.

But remember Sarah's response when the Lord told her and Abraham they would conceive a son at their age? "Shall I of a surety bear a child, which am old?" she asked (Genesis 18:13). Through His gentle rebuke, the Lord sent a message to each of us: "Is any thing too hard for the Lord?" (v. 14).

I am not expecting the miracle Sarah received. But I believe in miracles. I have seen miracles. I believe in the ministering of angels. I have experienced the reality of priesthood power. I have received revelation. And I believe the scripture is true, that we could just as likely stretch forth our puny arms and stop the Missouri River in its decreed course as "to hinder the Almighty from pouring down knowledge from heaven upon [us]" (Doctrine and Covenants 121:33).

In many ways, over many years, I have learned that the Lord will not fail us. I can't imagine how I would have handled so many years alone without the gospel of Jesus Christ. I haven't received everything I've asked for—yet—but the Lord has walked beside me and carried me a good part of the way. He has kept His promises to me.

My dear sisters, we are the most blessed of all women. We elected to come to earth and were then chosen to be here now during this exciting, culminating, climactic season. I pray that we will spare no effort to seek the breadth and depth of the Lord's exceeding, precious promises. As we do, we will have the ability to calm hearts, soothe fears, encourage others along the covenant path, testify boldly, and literally change lives in dynamic ways. We will be able to resist flattery and recognize truth. And we will excel in the great work of gathering, especially in gathering our families and friends.

May we "cheerfully do all things that lie in our power," and then "stand still, with the utmost assurance, to see the salvation of God, and for his arm to be revealed" (Doctrine and Covenants 123:17). For He reveals His arm by keeping His promises.

Notes

1. Russell M. Nelson, "Begin with the End in Mind," statement made from Salt Lake Temple on January 16, 2018.
2. See, for example, Tad Callister, "Our Identity and Our Destiny," BYU devotional, August 14, 2012.
3. Doctrine and Covenants 138:53, 55.
4. *Doctrines of the Restoration: Sermons & Writings of Bruce R. McConkie* [Salt Lake City: Bookcraft, 1989], 187–98.
5. Dallin H. Oaks, "Truth and Tolerance," BYU devotional, September 11, 2011.
6. Gary E. Stevenson, "Deceive Me Not," *Ensign*, November 2019.
7. Russell M. Nelson, "Revelation for the Church, Revelation for Our Lives," *Ensign*, May 2018.
8. Russell M. Nelson, "Spiritual Treasures," *Ensign*, November 2019.

INCREASING OUR CAPACITY TO RECOGNIZE AND RECEIVE REVELATION

TRACY BROWNING

I can remember, at sixteen, when the missionaries invited me to be baptized. After accepting that invitation and making preparations for that happy event, I was taught that following the ordinance of the baptism, a second priesthood ordinance would be performed that would confirm my membership in the Church and enable me to receive the gift of the Holy Ghost. In my limited understanding at the time, I anticipated that the moment hands were laid upon my head and the pronouncement to receive the Holy Ghost was made, I would experience a sort of physical or recognizable sensation as the Spirit of the Lord dwelt within me. I simply expected that from that point forward, the Holy Ghost and I would settle into a comfortable companionship—one that was easy to discern, always clear and effortless. But, on that day, there was no grand manifestation, no outwardly discernible difference in my sensitivities other than the feelings of peace, happiness, and reverence that came with making my first covenant with my Father in Heaven. I would soon come to learn that the Spirit of the Lord can often be subtle, quiet, and gentle in His ministering and messaging.

The reality of my relationship with the Holy Ghost moving forward from that day has been and continues to be an exercise in the tuning of my spiritual ears to better hear the voice of the Lord and His direction for my life, and the constancy and consistency of striving to keep my covenants to help reduce any barriers, within my control, that could create distance between me and the Spirit of God. Through spiritual growth and experience in the gospel I have gained a richer understanding of the gift that was bestowed on me because of my faithful step of baptism.

Elder David A. Bednar has taught:

> These four words—"Receive the Holy Ghost"—are not a passive pronouncement; rather, they constitute a priesthood injunction—an authoritative admonition to act and not simply to be acted upon (see 2 Nephi 2:26). The Holy Ghost does not become operative in our lives merely because hands are placed upon our heads and those four important words are spoken. As we receive this ordinance, each of us accepts a sacred and ongoing responsibility to desire, to seek, to work, and to so live that we indeed "receive the Holy Ghost" and its attendant spiritual gifts.[1]

President Russell M. Nelson's 2018 plea to the Church to "increase our spiritual capacity to receive revelation" and to "choose to do the spiritual work required to enjoy the gift of the Holy

Ghost, and hear the voice of the Spirit more frequently and more clearly"[2] has created an opportunity for me to examine what that spiritual work is that I could do to enlarge, to make more room, and to expand my spiritual capacity to recognize and receive the maximum amount of divine guidance possible in my life. And to achieve this I'm often searching for help in two areas:

1. Learning how to recognize the voice of the Lord.
2. Increasing my capacity to receive revelation.

Learning How to Recognize the Voice of the Lord

In that first pursuit, it's not uncommon along our spiritual journey to wonder if we really can recognize the voice of the Spirit and differentiate it from our natural conscience. We may wonder if there is a distinction, or if that distinction even matters. But because our desire and longing is to hear from God and to gain insight from His wisdom, for many this question may persist.

While some voices that speak clear opposition to the gospel of Jesus Christ may be easier to recognize, our own voice can, at times, be more difficult to distinguish from the Holy Ghost, and sometimes we are left wondering if a thought or a feeling is a prompting from the Spirit or a good idea born out of our own personal sentiments.

There are a few things that we can consider as we continue our personal journey to recognize how the voice of the Lord speaks to us.

First, the scriptures describe the voice of the Spirit as still and small. As we seek increased personal revelation it will be necessary for us to prioritize clearing away any "noise" in our minds that may make it difficult to hear the voice of the Lord. In our day-to-day lives we have a multitude of thoughts and feelings that we encounter. Taking purposeful steps toward creating a space for stillness within us, especially as we come before the Lord, seeking and searching for inspiration and guidance, will be an important step in recognizing God's voice.

Another way to help discern God's voice is to employ a modified version of the phrase "practice makes perfect" that I call "practice brings perspective." Choosing to consistently practice acting in faith on those good thoughts and feelings of which you may be questioning the origin can invite an ability to understand the voice of the Spirit in its true relation to other voices. Moroni taught, "Every thing which inviteth to do good, and to persuade to believe in Christ, is sent forth by the power and gift of Christ; wherefore ye may know with a perfect knowledge it is of God" (Moroni 7:16).

As you continually take faithful steps, the Lord can help you sort through and recognize His voice through a process of learning.

Some perspectives that I've learned about the voice of the Lord in my life through practice include that when the Spirit speaks:

- He testifies of Jesus Christ.
- He builds my faith on principles of the gospel.
- He confirms truth and my righteous choices.

- He calms and removes my fears.
- He encourages me to repent (and this is important) without condemnation.
- He sometimes prompts me to do things that are contrary to my own personal preference, rather than consistently confirming an action aligned to my strong desires.
- He speaks confidence about my spiritual talents.
- He provides warnings that help me navigate unsafe territory.

As a mother, I have experienced many times of seeking to understand whether some of my thoughts and feelings concerning my children or my family reflected my own sensibility or was a more specific message from the Lord. I'm sure this is not an unfamiliar wrestle for many mothers. I can recall one persistent thought that presented a very memorable desire for discernment between the two.

My husband and I had been married for about fourteen years at the time, and we had one child, our daughter who was eleven. Life was progressing as expected, but a thought began to take shape in my mind—one that I'd had previously, but this time with some new intensity that was unfamiliar. I could not stop thinking that it might be time for my husband and me to grow our family and make room for more children. As the thought increased in potency, I would at times wrestle to understand if this was guidance from the Spirit or if I was just manifesting unresolved feelings of guilt that my daughter was advancing in age, and so was I, and that some perceived window was closing on this opportunity to expand our family.

As I started to have conversations with my husband about what I was thinking and feeling and started to become settled with the idea of preparing to act on that sense, our family was then thrust into an unexpected trial, which resulted in our accepting legal care for the four-year-old son of a close family member. The next few years of this experience took all of our emotional and physical attention as we navigated the very challenging and serious circumstances of that placement. Those earlier thoughts of growing our family were quickly dispatched to the background as my husband and I focused our combined energy and faith on seeking earnest and pleading direction on how to help this very precious and beloved young boy who was in our care.

During this difficult time, there were, however, beautifully poignant moments in our home life, where we all felt an increase of joy, bonding, and completeness within our family that provided glimpses of a new but unclear future. The relationships that were being formed among us were quickly and surprisingly transforming into a unit that we all desired to be eternal. And after a long while, through many growing experiences, we found ourselves as a family in the house of the Lord being sealed to our son. And that question—about whether we should grow our family—returned to the foreground, and in the new light of experience and context, it became clear that the voice of the Lord had spoken early words of preparation to my mind and heart so that we as a family could see the work of His hand in all the places of our lives, at all varying times.

President Gordon B. Hinckley taught powerfully that the way to know the difference between the voice of the Lord and our own is ultimately to ask ourselves, "Does it persuade one to do good, to rise, to stand tall, to do the right thing, to be kind, to be generous?" because if it does, "then it is of the Spirit of God."[3]

Increasing Our Capacity to Receive Revelation

The Lord regularly uses a familiar pattern throughout scripture that often expresses three things:

1. Instruction on His nature.
2. Teachings or commands for our benefit.
3. Promised blessings.

I have found that not only recognizing this pattern but also utilizing it as a lens through which I view personal messages coming from God can help me to have greater spiritual strength. It has provided additional room in my spiritual reservoirs for the Spirit to reveal important truths to me.

As you pursue greater connection with our Savior Jesus Christ and seek to receive divine guidance from Him in your life, and as you encounter the voice of the Lord in your scripture study, on your knees through prayer, in studying the words of prophets, in your meetinghouses, in the voices of those the Lord sends to minister to you, and in His holy temple, I invite you to consistently ponder these three questions:

- How is God is inviting me to get to know Him?
- How is He seeking to build my trust and confidence in Him?
- How is God trying to bless me through my obedience to His promptings and counsel?

Each of these questions can help you to understand, give shape to, and provide greater influence on God's words in your life. In the Doctrine and Covenants the Lord teaches us, declaring, "Verily, verily, I say unto you, that assuredly as the Lord liveth, who is your God and your Redeemer, even so surely shall you receive a knowledge of whatsoever things you shall ask in faith, . . . believing that you shall receive" (Doctrine and Covenants 8:1).

How can each question bring an increased capacity for receiving revelation?

First, understanding that God can only be revealed through revelation invites us to prioritize in our lives the first great commandment, "Thou shalt love the Lord thy God with all thy heart, and with all thy soul, and with all thy mind" (Matthew 22:37).

Often, through personal revelation, God is seeking to show us that He knows us individually and intimately. There have been countless times in my life when the Spirit of the Lord has born witness of God's watchful eye over me, including at times when it has been more difficult for me to discover His presence on my own. Faithful disciples of our Savior would feel prompted to reach out to me to express love in ways that made bare its origins with God. Some of His sons and daughters would feel impressed to make inspired invitations that would prick my heart and again help me to recognize my Savior's voice. I will be eternally grateful for the ways that God reveals Himself and His intimate and individual love for me and for you. As the lyrics of a well-loved gospel hymn instruct, "His eye is on the sparrow, and I know He watches me."

Secondly, seeking to understand that God desires for us to have trust and confidence in Him can provide the help we need in receiving revelation through the Spirit. The Lord wants us to be assured in Him. He desires for us to exercise our faith in Him with confidence, demonstrating our belief and trust in Him even inasmuch to be "led by the Spirit, not knowing beforehand the things which [you] should do, nevertheless [going] forth" (1 Nephi 4:6–7).

As a new investigator to the Church, my mother reached a pivotal junction in her study of the restored gospel of Jesus Christ. She desired to know if the Book of Mormon was indeed the true word of God, as was testified to her by the missionaries, and if she should be baptized. After offering a sincere and pleading prayer to know the answers to her questions, she waited for God's reply.

Soon after her fervent prayer, God's voice was revealed in an unexpected and deeply sacred way. While it was clear that His response was evidence of His voice delivering a message to her, the content of His words did not directly nor precisely respond to her questions. So my mother was now presented with a choice: she could either put aside all the experiences that she'd had while reading the Book of Mormon and studying with the missionaries, where she'd felt good about what she was learning, or she could act in faith on the doctrine that she was being taught and demonstrate her trust in God. She knew that she could not deny the evidence that the Spirit of the Lord had presented, even though she did not fully understand it.

Gratefully, my mother turned her feet to the covenant path and made the decision to trust God and be baptized. Approximately two years later, with many learning and growing gospel experiences in between, my mother stood in the Washington D.C. Temple and presented herself to receive the gift of the Lord's endowment. As she committed herself to the Savior in these new covenants, the familiar voice of the Lord returned once again. He repeated the message from the night when she had offered that early prayer. She was astounded that it was now, a considerable time after those early faithful steps, that the confirmation she was seeking came.

God desires for us to build our trust and confidence in Him, and that can be demonstrated in our faithful actions even when the path is not fully illuminated. Sometimes the Lord responds to our enquiring with messages that reveal His priorities and perspectives, which may differ from our own. In the case of my mother, I believe that the Lord wanted to demonstrate that His preparations for her future discipleship expanded beyond what she was capable of understanding, but that if she was willing to act, even within the limits of her understanding, He would reward her faith.

Third, recognizing that God desires to bless us through our

willingness to be obedient can also bring increased spiritual capacity for revelation.

The Prophet Joseph Smith taught, "There is a law, irrevocably decreed in heaven before the foundations of this world, upon which all blessings are predicated—and when we obtain any blessing from God, it is by obedience to that law upon which it is predicated" (Doctrine and Covenants 130:20–21). Additionally, One of the most oft-repeated themes in the Book of Mormon is the principle that if we keep the commandments, we will prosper in the land.

God has promised that those who keep His commandments will receive the mysteries of His kingdom (see Doctrine and Covenants 63:23). Therefore, being obedient to God's commands is an important preparatory measure to receiving revelation. Through the process of repentance, clearing away any impediments in our lives that would prevent us from hearing the voice of the Lord is a critical step in attaining consistent guidance from God. Striving to keep the commandments and accepting the Lord's gentle and loving encouragements to be reconciled to Him through repentance will provide the Spirit with fertile ground to receive God's words.

Ask the Lord to illuminate any areas in your life that may be creating stumbling blocks to hear and receive His word. You need not be perfect to come before the Lord to ask for His help. As you commit yourself, prepare to receive more of His counsel into your life, and allow Him to prevail. He will instruct you in "all things what ye should do" (2 Nephi 32:3–5).

God's process of instruction is "line upon line, precept upon precept," and for those who "hearken unto [His] precepts," they will be "give[n] more" (2 Nephi 28:30). One experience that has demonstrated this principle of evolving revelation began a few years ago for me. I received a spiritual prompting that let me know that some changes were coming to my life, and those transitions would include some stretching, growing, and spiritual refinement. After receiving that message, I went about creating a checklist of every experience that I was having from that point forward. At the conclusion of each experience, I would put a mental tick-mark next to it and presume that this experience must surely be the fulfillment of that personal revelation. This went on for several years, with ever-evolving spiritual experiences that seemed to be stretching me and growing me, ofttimes with some discomfort. Finally, I returned to the Lord and asked when I would be able to cross off this revelation. The returned reply that I received from the Lord was simple: "There is no expiration date for revelation."

God's messages can continue to unfold over time, giving fuller and richer expression to each preceding message. Just like the preparatory prompting about the growth of my family, or my mother's narrowed answer to her prayer, this message from God about my personal discipleship took shape over a long time through small faithful steps that allowed for more of the path to be illuminated ahead.

I testify to you that our Savior Jesus Christ knows us individually and intimately. If we accept our prophet's earnest plea to increase our spiritual capacity to receive revelation, we will be able receive the necessary inspiration and divine guidance that is necessary for us to navigate life's challenges and opportunities.

Notes

1. David A Bednar, "Receive the Holy Ghost," *Ensign*, November 2010.
2. Russell M. Nelson, "Revelation for the Church, Revelation for Our Lives," *Ensign*, May 2018.
3. Gordon B. Hinckley, in *Preach My Gospel* (2004), 97.

PRACTICING PERFECTION

CAMILLE JOHNSON

For the last thirty-plus years I have been practicing law. I think there is a reason they refer to it as the practice of law.

I have never taken a perfect deposition, nor conducted a perfect cross-examination—there was always another question, or a better question I could have asked.

I have never written a perfect brief because, in retrospect, there was always a point I could have articulated with more clarity.

And I never presented perfect oral argument before a judge or justices. Almost always in the middle of the night after the argument, I thought of something really clever and persuasive I could have said.

But I believe the service I provided to my clients was not only satisfactory; it was of value. I was practicing law with an eye toward changing, improving, and perfecting. My efforts, though imperfect, were sufficient because I was practicing.

One of my best friends in the Book of Mormon is Sariah. I

am always delighted to read about her in 1 Nephi. I can identify with her. Her reactions ring true to me. Sariah practiced faith when she left Jerusalem, and her gold and silver, and took nothing with her into the wilderness except her family and a few needful provisions. Then, recall from chapter 3, Lehi dreamed a dream that the sons of Lehi and Sariah should return to Jerusalem to retrieve the brass plates from Laban.

By the time you get to 1 Nephi chapter 5, Sariah's sons had been gone for some time—we don't know for sure how long—but we know that they had traveled back to Jerusalem, gone home to load up all their precious things, and employed several strategies to get the plates from uncooperative Laban. And Sariah was concerned!

Sariah reacted the way I think I might have. She was worried about her sons, she mourned because of them, she complained a bit, and at one point she said something to Lehi she probably later regretted about him being a visionary man.

But Sariah practiced a little faith, she listened to the comforting words spoken to her by Lehi, she practiced patience, she practiced waiting on the Lord, she practiced supporting her husband, and when her sons returned with the plates of brass, her joy was full! And then she knew "of a surety" that they were on a mission from the Lord (1 Nephi 5:8). Her practiced faith was so keen, in fact, that she was willing to get on a ship, built by her sons who were not ship builders, to sail to an unknown destination, which turned out to be the promised land.

Sariah was practicing. She was practicing faith in the Lord

Jesus Christ and patience and long-suffering. She was practicing perfection.

We can be perfect in discreet tasks. For example, we can be perfect in reading from the Book of Mormon every day. We can pay our tithing with perfection. Or a piece of music can be played with precision, hitting every note. But I wonder if I musician who performs a piece of music without making a mistake still wonders if the right amount of emotion was expressed. To me it is the difference between mortal perfection—hitting every note right—and eternal perfection—creating a heavenly song. That heavenly song can only be played with and because of the Savior.

President Nelson has taught us, "Perfection is pending. It can come in full only after the Resurrection and only through the Lord. It awaits all who love Him and keep his commandments."[1]

In Moroni's final plea to us, he said, "Come unto Christ, and be perfected in him, and deny yourselves of all ungodliness; . . . love God with all your might, mind, and strength, then is his grace sufficient for you, that by his grace ye may be perfect in Christ" (Moroni 10:32–33).

Remember the brother of Jared and his people, who were directed to build barges according to the instructions of the Lord? The barges were small, light on the water, and tight like a dish.

And in an act of tremendous faith, those Jaredites got in the barges they built and "many times [were] buried in the . . . sea, because of the . . . waves which broke upon them, and . . . the wind did never cease to blow . . . while they were upon the waters" until after 344 days they arrived at the promised land (Ether 6:6–8).

But recall that before the Jaredites got into the barges for the promised land, while they were traveling in the wilderness, they "did build barges, in which they did cross many waters, being directed continually by the hand of the Lord" (Ether 2:6). They had been practicing barge building and practicing faith in the Lord before their 344-day journey began. Of course, the Lord could have led them around those bodies of water while they were traveling in the wilderness. But He didn't! He let them practice barge building, and importantly, He gave them opportunities to practice their faith in Him. I think their practice prepared them for that very long journey to the promised land.

We are practicing perfection to return to our heavenly home. And the Savior, whose grace makes eternal perfection possible, gives us opportunities to practice.

Perfection, mortal and eternal, is our objective. Practice makes perfect with the Savior. He makes all the difference. President Nelson has counseled us: "Let us do the best we can and try to improve each day. When our imperfections appear we can keep trying to correct them. We can be more forgiving of flaws in ourselves and among those we love. We can be comforted and forbearing."[2]

Sisters, keep practicing! Our dear prophet has reminded us, "The Lord loves effort, because effort brings rewards that can't come without it."[3]

I testify that the Lord loves you and wants you to return home. Perfection is pending in Him and with Him.

Notes

1. Russell M. Nelson, "Perfection Pending," *Ensign*, November 1995.
2. Russell M. Nelson, "Perfection Pending."
3. Russell M. Nelson, in Joy D. Jones, "An Especially Noble Calling," *Ensign*, May 2020.